Flourish

GO DEEP. TAKE ROOT.
REMAIN STEADFAST.

NATALIE MAKI

WESTBOW
PRESS®
A DIVISION OF THOMAS NELSON
& ZONDERVAN

NIV: Unless otherwise specified scriptures are taken from the Holy Bible,
New International Version. NIV. Copyright 1973, 1978, 1984 by International
Bible Society. Used by permission of Zondervan. All rights reserved.

AMP: Scripture quotations marked AMP are from The Amplified Bible, Old Testament copyright
1965, 1987 by the Zondervan Corporation. The Amplified Bible, New Testament copyright
1954, 1958, 1987 by The Lockman Foundation. Used by permission. All rights reserved.

ESV: Unless otherwise indicated, all scripture quotations are from The Holy
Bible, English Standard Version (ESV). Copyright 2001 by Crossway Bibles, a
division of Good News Publishers. Used by permission. All rights reserved.

NLT: Scripture quotations marked NLT are taken from the Holy Bible, New
Living Translation, copyright 1996, 2004, 2007. Used by permission of Tyndale
House Publishers, Inc. Carol Stream, Illinois 60188. All rights reserved.

KJV: Scripture quotations taken from the King James Version of the Bible.

RSV: Scripture quotations marked RSV are taken from the Revised Standard Version
of the Bible, copyright 1946, 1952, 1971 by the Division of Christian Education of the
National Council of the Churches of Christ in the USA. Used by permission.

WestBow Press books may be ordered through booksellers or by contacting:

WestBow Press
A Division of Thomas Nelson & Zondervan
1663 Liberty Drive
Bloomington, IN 47403
www.westbowpress.com
1 (866) 928-1240

Because of the dynamic nature of the Internet, any web addresses or links contained in
this book may have changed since publication and may no longer be valid. The views
expressed in this work are solely those of the author and do not necessarily reflect the
views of the publisher, and the publisher hereby disclaims any responsibility for them.

Any people depicted in stock imagery provided by Thinkstock are models,
and such images are being used for illustrative purposes only.
Certain stock imagery © Thinkstock.

ISBN: 978-1-5127-8085-7 (sc)
ISBN: 978-1-5127-8087-1 (hc)
ISBN: 978-1-5127-8086-4 (e)

Library of Congress Control Number: 2017904484

Print information available on the last page.

WestBow Press rev. date: 04/14/2017

For Anna, Melody, Beth, Irene, and Penelope.

To my sweet husband, thank you for the simplicity and constancy of your Genesis 24:67 love.

For my little e-mail list, "Ladies Loving the Lord." Thank you for listening.

To my editors—thank you, thank you, thank you for making this book what it has become, for your dear friendship, and for your unwavering encouragement.

Contents

Remain Steadfast.

Foreword by Hayley Darden

As a 30 year-old single New Yorker, I find the circumstances in the Psalms a bit difficult to relate to. I don't often flee pagan militaries or hide in solid rocks. Yet the timeless emotions captured in the Psalms still resonate, even in my chaotic city life. Like David, I struggle to remember that I can't measure my worth by how I look or by what I've achieved. In short, I flee from Marie Claire headlines like "Never, Ever Age" and into friendships with people steeped in God's Word.

That's who Natalie is to me. I'm not afraid to tell her the darkest of my thoughts or the worst of my deeds. I can count on her to laugh and cry with me through dating stories, struggles with envy, fevers of lust, and flus of shame. And, when we're done, she makes me less afraid to "taste and see that the Lord is good."

About three years ago, awash in desperate frustration, Natalie came to a breaking point in her faith. Somewhere between studying for the bar exam and fruitlessly searching for a job, she snapped. And in doing so, she got really, really honest with the Lord. Mostly, she told him she was kind of mad that life wasn't easy and that she was tired of being disappointed. But more than that, she challenged him to show up.

And you know what—he did. God made himself tangibly, palpably known to Natalie in the Word, and even through mundane things like cooking dinner. As he revealed himself, she started to experience everything that hurt as a place she could expect God to show up and do some radical healing. Little by little, she became the sort of woman who could write the short and beautiful book that you're holding in your hands.

Sometimes, it seems like these noticeably "extra-spiritual" people like the woman I've just described become inwardly beautiful but suddenly lose all connection with the material reality the rest of us are trapped in. But that's why I want you to know that learning how good God truly is not only made Natalie's heart more beautiful— it also made her actual real-live-made-of-human-skin face more beautiful. Truly, the more she trusts the Lord, her countenance actually *glows*. I swear, she increasingly looks like a teenager in love or a twenty-something whose only responsibility is to brunch and try on resort wear. I'm not sure whether I'd call this a "Jesus facial" or a "spiritual tan." In any case, it signals the kind of health, life, and vitality I'm often afraid to believe God offers.

About eighteen months ago, Natalie and I began a new season of our friendship when I moved from our nation's capital to the Big Apple. Our lives look very different but our hearts are still the same. She's been married for more than seven years and is a California-based stay-at-home mom and part-time boss-lady lawyer. I live in a room about the size of a festival port-o-potty in one of New York's hippest neighborhoods and collect eclectic friends and experiences while trying to advance my career and get excited about a second date. We're both learning that love—whether you're married or single or whether you're a Christian or not—always requires a death to self. Love requires self-extension. We're also learning to experience God as *abundantly good, regardless of our circumstances*.

It can be tough to remember just how good God is, but friends like Natalie challenge me to dig in and pursue discovering more of his character. She's my spiritual half-way house. In addition to my latest insights and my funniest stories, our friendship is a place where

I share the moments that are hard. Over text threads and late night calls, my darkest thoughts, ugliest deeds, deepest griefs, and my most stubborn discontents give way to the truth that experiencing God in each moment tastes better than either of us dared imagine.

This book is an invitation. It's an invitation from Natalie, but really, it's an invitation from an intoxicatingly wonderful God. I hope this book will become to you what our friendship has been to me—a place that warms your heart and loosens your soul until you dare to taste and believe that our God really, really is *always* just that good.

Introduction: The Little Yellow House on Kramer

Flourish: to grow luxuriantly, or thrive in growth, as a plant.[1]

But I am like an olive tree flourishing in the house of God; I trust in God's unfailing love for ever and ever. I will praise you forever for what you have done; in your name I will hope, for your name is good. I will praise you in the presence of your saints. (Psalm 52:8–9 NIV Life Application Study Bible)

The Lord will guide you always; he will satisfy your needs in a sun-scorched land and will strengthen your frame. You will be like a well-watered garden, like a spring whose waters never fail. (Isaiah 58:11)

And I pray that you, being rooted and established in love, may have power, together with all the Lord's holy people, to grasp how wide and long and high and deep is the love of Christ, and to know this love that surpasses knowledge—that you may be filled

---

[1] "Flourish." www.dictionary.com (Accessed May 13, 2016,)

to the measure of all the fullness of God. (Ephesians 3:17–19)

I live in the little yellow house on Kramer Street in Washington, DC. Years ago, before God ever put the dream of writing in my heart, I used to compose sentences about my day as I fell asleep at night. I imagined the title of these non sequitur essays might be, "The Little Yellow House on Kramer," because (a) that's where I live; and (b) I'm not that original when it comes to titles.

This house has been an unexpected gift—the most perfect place for us in ways we never could have anticipated. The Lord has rooted us in this home. We've cursed the miniscule countertops, moaned about city rats, the mosquitoes, and the piles of mattresses in the vacant lot, and grumbled about the crazy that is the 4th of July in DC. Still, this home has become a sacred place. The little yellow house on Kramer is full of memories, laughter, friends, and big and small moments alike. We have the tiniest of white picket fences, but to me, it counts as living the dream. Here, in the midst of chaotic city life, fire trucks, sirens, construction jackhammering, and ubiquitous and indiscriminate yelling at all hours of the day and night (seriously, what is the deal with that?!), we have our own small haven.

This morning, I woke up a few precious minutes before my daughter, Penny. I made coffee, wrapped a blanket around my shoulders, and sat on our front step to greet the day. The block was quiet, the sky full of rain, but the birds were up and flitting about, exhilarated by the shift in season. It's spring in DC and the city is showing off. Our rose bush, a scrawny bunch of sticks when we first moved in, is lush and leafy and bursting with buds about to pop in a pink and glorious display. Over the years, we've wired the branches to the front of our house and now scores of blooms sit right under our bedroom window.

Sitting on the front step, the view over the top of the fence is dominated by a massive and regal ginkgo tree. We live in the middle of a cluster of three little one-way streets. Each street is lined with ginkgo trees varying in size and gender. The trees turn a fiery, brilliant yellow in the fall. After the peak of color, the leaves fall gently to the ground and the sidewalks become carpeted and soft. It feels like walking the yellow brick road in Oz.

Our ginkgo is the tallest and sturdiest on the block. His bark is deeply creviced, with elegant gnarls and the distinguished gray of a tree who knows his place in the world. I like to think of him as a sentinel, guarding our home, providing protection, shade, covering, and a strong presence. Even though I love a good foray into anthropomorphism, in this case, I can actually say our ginkgo is a male. If you're not familiar with ginkgo trees, trust me, you want a male ginkgo growing in front of your house.

He's grown quite a bit since we moved in. As his branches reach higher into the sky and spread out to cover us, his roots are growing deep and wide. When the wind whips down the street and the sideways rain threatens our tenuous power connection, his roots hold him steadfast. The deeper the roots, the sturdier the tree. A healthy root system means a healthy tree. To walk as strong, faithful women by the power of the Holy Spirit, we need to be *rooted* in the Word of God. Roots don't grow overnight. It's a slow and steady process of water, nutrients, sunlight, and time.

This book chronicles my own slow and steady process of becoming rooted in the Lord through the study of his Word. These pages are a journey into the interiors of my life, an invitation to join me in the messy yet holy work God is doing in my heart. These last few years, God has helped me ditch my "when is the other shoe going to drop theology," tackle my anger and my worry, and helped me make peace with my capacity. He's teaching me to make space for rest and Sabbath. He's giving me a more gracious understanding of hospitality and he's showing me the power of persevering in prayer.

Each time I've accepted his invitation to deal with my envy, my media consumption, or my pride, I've become a little freer to live as my created self. Each time I've said "yes" to his work, I've become a little more of the woman he intended. I am not a theologian. I am a mom and a wife, a daughter and a granddaughter, a neighbor and a friend. Yet in my small and ordinary life, in the dark corners, in the dead of night, and in the sunshine, I have seen "the goodness of the Lord in the land of the living" (Psalm 27:13). It is heaven to behold. I want more of it. I want it for you, for me, for our children, and our families. "Taste and see that the Lord is good, blessed is the man who takes refuge in him" (Psalm 34:8).

Go Deep.

The Interiors

You have searched me, Lord, and you know me. You
know when I sit and when I rise; you perceive my
thoughts from afar. You discern my going out and
my lying down; you are familiar with all my ways.
Before a word is on my tongue you, Lord, know it
completely. (Psalm 139:1–4)

Initially, I floated the idea of titling this book *The Interiors* to
my husband, and he informed me that it sounded like a creepy,
depressing movie. This apparently menacing term occurred to me
while I was struggling to find the words to describe my curiosities.
I was trying to explain to a friend that I just didn't think I was cut
out for working in an office and staring at a computer screen all day.

In professional settings, I always feel like I'm faking it. I try to
be professional and talk about professional things, and I pretend to
be formal and reserved. In my head (and all too often out loud), I'm
longing to talk about the interiors of people's lives. I want to know
what makes them tick, what they eat for breakfast, what their kids
are like, and how they spend their Saturdays. I want to know how
they met their spouses, what they like to read, and if they're happy in
their lives. In short, I want to know everything personal and nothing
professional. I am obsessed with the interiors of a person.

When I started my first job as an exuberant twenty-two-year-old,

I was overly enthusiastic about everything, with appallingly lax filters for every thought that popped into my head. I worked in government and public affairs, and a lot of my job involved meeting people and talking to them about our company's products. I met lots of new people (new people are an especial favorite of mine—so much to learn!) often in awkward trade show settings.

At each event, I would chat up potential clients all day long. I did this mostly to entertain myself, saving my sanity in the suffocating boredom and taking my mind away from my aching feet. My very patient boss would go to other meetings or take calls and come back and ask me, "So what do they think about our product? Do they think the legislature will take up any public safety issues this session?" And I'd say, "Uh, well, we didn't quite get there, but I can tell you his wife's name, how many kids he has, where he vacations each summer, his favorite food, and what sports he played in high school."

The interiors—that's the stuff I care about, and that's where my mind, heart, and conversations go like they're following a siren call. They're what I'm always thinking about and what I like to write about. I've made peace with the fact that the interiors are my jam. I never liked wearing suits anyway.

The interiors are also where God does much of his work in us. He speaks to us in the morning quiet before the bustling day begins, his voice a tender whisper that transcends whatever limited time we dedicate to devotions. He longs to be invited into our interiors, to make the inmost parts of us beautiful, renewed, and holy. He desires that we have rich inner lives, inquiring minds, and settled spirits. When we invite him into our interiors, our days become marked by steady dialogue with him. We begin, as he always intended, to see him in everything. He smiles at us through the eyes of a giggling baby; he ministers to us through our closest relationships. When we invite him into our interiors, we encounter the living God, the "Father of all, who is over all and through all and in all" (Ephesians 4:6).

A Rod of Steel

Being confident of this, that he who began a good work in you will carry it on to completion until the day of Christ Jesus. (Philippians 1:6).

Taste and see that the Lord is good; blessed is the one who takes refuge in him. (Psalm 34:8)

He has made everything beautiful in its time. He has also set eternity in the heart of man; yet no one can fathom what God has done from beginning to end. (Ecclesiastes 3:11)

It's a frigid Tuesday. I'm writing this from my bed. Sam, our dog, is curled up under the covers, the heating pad is toasting my toes, and I'm wearing the lipstick jammies I got for Christmas. I'm running on a frightfully small amount of sleep; the tiny baby razor teeth slicing through Penny's gums have utterly derailed our attempts at rest.

This weekend I had a lovely chat with a friend about *using* the time when we're in a season of waiting, anticipation, lack, or pain. Although she and I are longing for different things, we feel that the Lord is calling us to rise above the fray and enter into his purpose for this moment in our lives.

Our conversation reminded me of a very painful but incredibly redemptive season when the Lord "put a rod of steel" in my spine. The experience was raw, difficult, and painful. But it was the beginning of something great. Almost three years ago on a cold, dark March morning, I found myself face down on my couch with a blanket pulled over my head, weeping uncontrollably and inconsolably while the song *More than Watchmen Wait for Morning* played over and over and over again. Sam stared at me perplexedly, an alarmed question in his soulful brown eyes. It's an ugly place to be when even your dog thinks you've lost it. Why, you might ask, was I having a certifiably crazy episode on my couch with only Sam as a witness?

On the morning in question, I was addled from a visit from a friend whose 4:00 a.m. airport pickup didn't show up, so I had taken her to catch an early-morning flight. This friend, bless her heart, came to visit at a very bad time. I was in my third year of law school and was desperately trying to find some gainful employment. She came to stay with us for five days to do interviews in DC. She went to law school in a different state but somehow had millions more connections and interviews *in my hometown*, and watching her leave my house every day in her suit to go live the life I wanted to live just pushed me over the edge. I kept it together while she was here, but I was *done*. And that morning, at 5:30 a.m., I finally broke before the Lord.

I was reeling with jealousy that the pieces were not coming together for me. I had received numerous rejection e-mails from job after job, which was only slightly better than the countless number of firms from which I never heard anything back. I didn't know what I wanted to do with my law degree; I was staring down the barrel of the California bar exam, and it seemed like everyone around me was getting job offers like crazy and moving on to pursue their happy, successful lives. I was unbelievably frustrated. I did everything "right." I slogged through law review, giving up weekends to check citations for sixty-page journal articles. I worked hard to get good grades, outlining months and months of reading material to make sure I scored well on exams, but it was to no avail. I was done, and I wanted out. My heart ached to move home to California because I believed the lie that getting out of DC would fix everything. I believed that changing the scenery would make my heart whole.

That gray morning, I wept and prayed. I could no longer hold on to the idols of success and achievement. I had to release my failure, the crippling disappointment, and the crushing doubt. That morning was the climax of a battle that had been waging in my spirit for a long time. I didn't let go because I wanted to; I didn't let go because I realized that God was in control, and I didn't let go because I made a conscious choice. I didn't have a choice. I was compelled to release what I thought my life should look like because I couldn't continue on in the fear, anxiety, and self-doubt.

Broken and bruised, I began a journey with the Lord from which I will never look back. Months later when I was recounting this experience to our pastor's wife, she looked at me with her wise, kind eyes and said, "Ah, he put a rod of steel in you. Every good woman needs that. It can never be taken away from you." A rod of steel is a life-altering encounter with God, after which your faith will never be the same. He might give you a rod of steel through an outrageous miracle or a longed-for answer to prayer. My rod of steel looked like an intense season of diving into God's Word, getting to know his character, and absorbing his promises in every corner of my soul.

From that fateful morning on, I tried to do things differently. I spent less time doing informational interviews, filling out job applications, and stressing. I spent more time in the Word—*much more* time in the Word. I graduated and studied my buns off for the bar exam, but I still didn't have a job or even any prospects in sight.

As all my peers headed off to fancy new jobs in gleaming offices,

I headed … to my couch. My mentor, Irene, had been praying for me, and she said, "Natalie, I really feel like you are to treat this time like a gift, and that you're supposed to use it to focus on time with the Lord and he will take care of your job." So I spent time with the Lord. I spent that fall and early winter doing three-hour devotions almost every morning. Then I spent my afternoons meeting with people or applying for jobs. At first I could barely focus for more than fifteen minutes, but as I spent more and more time with God and studying his Word (I even got myself a commentary), I found that he was completely changing our relationship.

Now it wasn't all spiritual mountaintops and roses. It was *hard*, and I needed that extended time with the Lord in the mornings to even make it out of bed. I needed the Lord to sustain me in a way I had never experienced. I started each morning in the depths of despair, and by the time I finished my devotions, I was at least up to ground zero.

What had seemed like a waste, a humiliation, and an unnecessary delay became a glorious opportunity. I began to experience the season as the gift it was intended to be for my soul. Seriously, when do you get six whole months to spend in the Word like it's your job? Let me tell you what God did in that time: he completely reoriented my faith. He became my anchor. He showed me that he is loving, good, and trustworthy in ways I had known in my head but never experienced in my heart. He showed me that he is my *Provider*.

After he put a rod of steel in me, I exited that season upright and supported, unalterably rooted in his Word. As hard as it was, I wouldn't trade that season. What he gave me in that time no one can ever take away from me. No circumstance, no grief, no loss, no challenge can undo what he did. I'm thirty years old. There will inevitably be difficult times ahead. Yet I know that my God loves me, that he is for me, and that he is working on my behalf, even when it doesn't feel like it. So, when hard things happen, and they most certainly will, "I am pressed but not crushed, persecuted, but not abandoned, struck down but not destroyed" (2 Corinthians 4:9).

My banner verse in that season was Psalm 119 (below). Have you ever really dug into Psalm 119? It is a treasure! It's the longest Psalm in the Bible. In it, David extols the word of the Lord, he praises God's law, vowing throughout to "meditate on your precepts, and consider your ways, to delight in your decrees; I will not neglect your word."

During that time, I wrote out Psalm 119:25–32:

> I am laid low in the dust;
> Preserve my life according to your word.
> I recounted my ways and you answered me;
> Teach me your decrees
> Let me understand the teaching of your precepts;
> Then I will meditate on your wonders.
> My soul is weary with sorrow,
> Strengthen me according to your word.
> Keep me from deceitful ways;
> Be gracious to me through your laws.
> I hold fast to your statutes, O Lord.
> Do not let me be put to shame.
> I run in the path of your commands,
> For you have set my heart free.

When we are weary with sorrow, the Lord strengthens us with his Word. He will not let us be put to shame. How beautiful is this image: "I run in the path of your commands, for you have set my heart free?" I want my heart to be free. I want to run in that freedom down the path he has lovingly laid out for me.

Whatever season you're in, I want to encourage you to *use* it. Instead of hating it or fighting it or running from it, try, as Sheryl Sandberg would say, *leaning in* to what the Lord is doing. He will meet you there. He will not leave you ashamed.

He is and always will be doing good work in us. He will carry these works to completion in Jesus Christ. If you find yourself in one of these painful waiting periods, ask the Lord to *redeem the time.* He will never leave you disappointed. You never know, he just might put a rod of steel in you.

The Word of God

In the beginning was the Word and the Word was with God and the Word was God. (John 1:1)

Out of the overflow of the heart, the mouth speaks. (Luke 6:45(b))

Washington, DC is digging itself out of two feet of snow, but it's sunny and gorgeous outside. I'm pleased to report this is the most I've ever enjoyed snow in regular life. Growing up in California, snow was a delightful rarity reserved for weekend trips to go sledding, skiing, to drink hot cocoa, and to indulge in the requisite après ski hot tub to soothe sore muscles.

Then I moved to Chicago and There. Was. So. Much. Snow. I could not get my head around the fact that people were still supposed to conduct their daily life ... in so much snow. During my first snow at Wheaton, I dressed for class in head-to-toe ski gear like I was hitting the slopes. I had my snow pants on and even had my ski goggles in my book bag because that's what you wear in the snow, right? Nope. Everyone else was wearing colorful pea coats, glossy leather riding boots, artfully perched slouchy snow hats, (I still can't figure out how to wear those things, how do they not fall off your head?) and brightly striped scarves. Yet, there I was, trekking to class like I was going to climb Everest after Philosophy 101.

Bottom line, snow still boggles my mind. We're supposed to go to work? In the snow? To the grocery store? To any place at all? People drive their cars in the snow?! What?!?!?!

But this time, I'm actually enjoying it. We had the weekend to be cozy inside together. Saturday was like a get out of jail free card to devour back-to-back Harry Potter movies, binge-watch Gilmore Girls, and eat half a pan of brownies by myself! The city was so quiet and peaceful. No cars on the road, no yelling in the streets. The pure, cleansing white of fresh snow blanketed our dirty city, making all things new. And then, the post-blizzard after-party! Snow brings out so much neighborliness and good cheer. Everyone was digging out the sidewalks and each others' cars. Lincoln Park was a veritable madhouse of puppies, babies, sledding, cross-country skiers, and rosy-cheeked, white-dusted football players. It was magical.

Just as snow blankets the streets outside, the Word of God is beginning to cover and protect my heart. After that ugly-face, can't breathe-hysterical crying on my couch, I arose furious, yet determined. I thought, "I'm going to know you God, because there doesn't seem to be any other way around it." I opened my Bible at the beginning and I started to read.

I was 27 years old. I had been a professing Christian my whole life. I attended Christian school for the better part of my education, yet I had never read the entire Bible end-to-end. It was time. In law school, you develop incredible critical thinking skills (while simultaneously becoming convinced of the utter, total depravity of mankind, and irrationally suspicious of everyone and everything). But still, you learn to sift, sort, and organize information in a logical, fact-based way. I turned my newly critical eye to Scripture and said, "Ok, God, let's see what you've got. I want to know what this is all about. The *whole shebang*, not just bits and pieces." That was almost three years ago. This has not been a "read the Bible in one year" endeavor, but a slow and steady progress. I'm almost finished with the Old Testament. I continue to read and re-read the Psalms daily because my heart needs the encouragement, and I'm currently in the book of Acts, which is quite a page-turner.

Unsurprisingly, the Lord has met me graciously in this quest. He turned my petulant temper tantrum into a thirst to know him, and gave me a rooted appreciation for his Word. He has drawn me deeper into relationship with him than I ever thought possible. It is intoxicating, in the way that only truth can be. It is life, for "in him we live and move and have our being" (Acts 17:28). Am I preaching to the choir? Maybe. Perhaps you know God, walk with him daily, and profess him as Lord and Savior. And yet … and yet … Do we not benefit from a reminder to pursue his Word? To soak it up every single day? I love to recall what my grandmother says about being in the Word daily, "We all need the Word of God every day: it is cleansing, it is life-giving and necessary. Just as we drink 8 glasses of water daily for our health, so we renew our souls with the refreshing water of life in the Word."

The verse *"Out of the overflow of the heart, the mouth speaks,"* has an interesting application to our knowledge and study of the Bible. I have occasionally heard it referenced in a negative context, for example, be mindful of what comes out of your mouth, because it reveals what's really going on in your heart. This is certainly true, but the Lord brought this verse to mind because I think it equally applies to our discipline of hiding his Word in our hearts. "I have hidden your word in my heart, that I might not sin against thee" (Psalm 119:11). If our hearts are filled with the Word of God, if the pathways of our mind are lined with his promises, then our mouths will speak his Word—in prayer, in conversation, in moments of doubt and struggle.

My mentor coined a term she likes to call lie replacement therapy. Lie replacement therapy is the practice of combating the lies of the enemy with the truth of Scripture. We counteract what the enemy wants us to believe about ourselves or a situation by speaking and believing God's truth. When we speak and pray scripture over ourselves, we interrupt the pathways in our minds, redirecting our thoughts, breaking the downward spiral. "For the word of God is living and active and sharper than any two-edged sword" (Hebrews 4:12). When we replace lies of the enemy and lies in our heads with the truth of God, something powerful happens. We actually rewire the way we think. We interrupt the pattern. We disrupt the status quo.

For example, if I'm struggling with envy, I will call to mind and meditate on verses that combat envy, such as Psalm 4:7, "You have given me greater joy than those who have abundant harvests of grain and new wine," to remind me of the truth that my ultimate home is in Jesus and *he* is my exceedingly great reward (New Living Translation).

The only way we can fight the enemy with the truth of Scripture is if we have the Word of God *in us.* Deep in our hearts. Residing in our souls. As our hearts become full of his words and his promises, our mouths will speak that truth. The Word of God will come to our minds swiftly, an ever-present help in times of trouble. "God is our refuge and strength, a very present help in trouble" (Psalm 46:1). But the Word of God cannot come to us swiftly if it's not in us. If we haven't taken the time to know him through his Word then we won't have it at the ready when we need it.

The Bible is a quirky book, filled with deeply flawed characters perpetually pursued by a holy God. Through the stories of his people, God's lovingkindness is revealed, and we begin to know the contours of his character like we know the backs of our own hands.

There are so many ways to be in the Word. My husband, Pete, is currently using Nicky Gumble's Bible in One Year app to do his devotions. It's been great, especially because it has an audio feature where Nicky Gumble and his wife, Pippa, read you devotions in their British accents. Sometimes at the end of our day, it makes us feel a little bit like Jesus and Mary Poppins are tag teaming putting us to bed. Last night, Nicky Gumble was sharing how we all want to hear the voice of God. But this can't happen if we don't *listen* for the voice of God. Moreover, *one of the main ways to hear the voice of God is to read his Word!*

God has given us **66 BOOKS and 1,281 PAGES** of his Word! We can't complain about not knowing God or not hearing from him if we haven't taken the time to read his Word. Like I discovered three years ago, and wish I had known earlier, the Lord can be found in his Word. He will not disappoint you.

Let's look at a few verses that highlight what God says about his Word:

> For the word of God is alive and active. Sharper than any double-edged sword, it penetrates even to dividing soul and spirit, joints and marrow; it judges the thoughts and attitudes of the heart. (Hebrews 4:12)

> So shall my word be that goeth forth out of my mouth: it shall not return unto me void, but it shall accomplish that which I please, and it shall prosper in the thing whereto I sent it. (Isaiah 55:11 KJV)

> So Jesus said to the Jews who had believed him, "If you abide in my word, you are truly my disciples, and you will know the truth, and the truth will set you free." (John 8:32)

> Again, the kingdom of heaven is like a merchant seeking beautiful pearls, who, when he had found

one pearl of great price, went and sold all that he had and bought it. (Matthew 13:45–46)

My son, if you accept my words and store up my commands within you, turning your ear to wisdom and applying your heart to understanding— indeed, if you call out for insight and cry aloud for understanding, and if you look for it as for silver and search for it as for hidden treasure, then you will understand the fear of the Lord and find the knowledge of God. (Proverbs 2:1–11)

The law of the Lord is perfect, refreshing the soul. The statutes of the Lord are trustworthy, making wise the simple. (Psalm 19:7)

The Word of God is living, active, perfect, refreshing, beautiful, and trustworthy. God's word accomplishes the purposes of his heart.

If you're not familiar with Fanny Crosby, her story is incredible. One of America's most gifted and prolific hymn writers, she was blinded in infancy, yet went on to become a powerful preacher and evangelical leader. When she was a child, her grandmother and a family friend took a special interest in teaching her Bible verses, encouraging her to memorize the entire Bible. This firm biblical foundation became the fount from which her beautiful hymns flowed. She was full to the brim and overflowing with the word of God. My prayer is that you would become deeply rooted in the word of God, and that his words would flow out of your mouth to bless and give life to others.

Set a Guard Over My Mouth

Set a guard over my mouth, O Lord;
Keep watch over the door of my lips.
Let not my heart be drawn to what is evil,
To take part in wicked deeds." (Psalm 141:3–4)

Bless and do not curse. (Romans 12:14)

Set me free from my prison, that I may praise your name.
(Psalm 142:7)

It's Monday. I've decided that Mondays are my stay-at-home, GSD (get stuff done) days and it has been enormously helpful to have a rhythm for accomplishing tasks. Usually, all I have to show for my Mondays is laundry, but my laundry is actually getting folded these days instead of living in a giant pile on my guest bed.

Last night the Lord prompted me to write about *it* and then he gave me the perfect devotional this morning about *it*—so with that as confirmation (if not a divine mandate), I'm going to eat some humble pie and tell you about *it:* my royal, very public, and embarrassing meltdown at Eastern Market, a local outdoor farmer's market in our neighborhood. The phrase from Psalm 141:3-4 "set a guard over my mouth" kept coming up in my quiet times last week and I thought, "Oh, what a nice verse, I'll have to remember that for some distant time in the future when I need to guard my mouth." Ha.

Since we may not be intimately acquainted with one another, perhaps I've managed to hold it together in front of you, and you may not know that I struggle with anger. God made me spicy, and most of the time, I like the facets of my personality this spiciness brings out. I am passionate. This is a descriptor I prefer over "intense," which, my friend pointed out, is an intense thing to say—specifying which adjective you prefer. Maybe I should just embrace intense. I experience high highs and low lows; I *feel* things deeply, which is sometimes complicated, but overall, the way I would prefer to live.

What is not so lovely is the anger that has accompanied my personality for most of my life. I have had some pretty mortifying moments, including screaming at my mom disrespectfully in front of my college roommates while driving the wrong direction on the Golden Gate Bridge trying, unsuccessfully, to get to a Giants game. Major fail. This is a moment I am *not* proud of and wish we could all forget.

You see, all of those normally nice emotions swimming inside of my head can be whipped into a white-hot fury at lightning speed. My heart starts beating wildly, a thousand hurtful words come to my mind, I stop caring what anyone thinks of me, and I desperately want to throw things. I'm not saying I get this angry very often or every time, just that I have the capacity for it. This is not the case for many people I know, including my darling, sweet husband. They just don't have it in them. I wish I were like that.

My Dad, who is pretty much me in a male body, or I guess I'm him in a female body, has been wonderfully gentle and instructive, working with me on my anger since I was a girl. He too has struggled with anger and the Holy Spirit has done some remarkable work in him. I've asked the Lord to work on my anger a lot over the years, and I can see his faithfulness to me in this area. My family has been the arbiter and witness of this process, God bless them.

I'm angry a whole lot less these days, and life is pretty marvelous. I've been surprised at how few times I've been truly angry since having a baby, even though I never sleep. It helps to have margin in my life, to spend time in the cleansing Word, and to be diligent about rest and Sabbath. All of these things make me less angry.

Sometimes, I even get wooed into thinking I'm done with it ... until I absolutely lose it and it feels like I'm right back at square one. I feel dirty and messy and so angry at myself for failing again in such a classic, Natalie way. It's like, geez, get it together!! You're thirty!! You have a child!! Be a grown up!!!! Stop using so many exclamation marks!!!!!!

Back to the meltdown. I played the magnanimous, loving wife and let Pete sleep in, getting up with Penny at 5:50 a.m. even after she woke up twice and I was exhausted. (Note: he almost always lets me sleep on the weekends, so his sleep-in was well overdue). Penny and I played, we ate breakfast, we read, I had seven cups of coffee and then I put her down for a nap.

At this point it was only 8:00 a.m., and our church was having a morning prayer meeting before the service to pray for international missionaries. Ordinarily, I eschew morning prayer meetings because I hate being anywhere in the morning at a particular time (personal point of growth recognized). But yesterday, I was feeling all awesome about myself, and maybe even a little holy, so I decided to go. To add to my slight sense of superiority, I dressed up like a real person, *in bootie heels*, and my favorite fall pencil skirt. Sporting my leather jacket, I *walked* to church, saying, "Good morning," to all the people I encountered and feeling great about life.

Church was lovely. Pete came to meet me with Penny, she had a great nap, he felt incredible from finally sleeping, and Penny was a doll in the service. We were firing on all cylinders. After the service,

I was starving because breakfast was a million hours ago and things started to go downhill.

I was fantasizing about lunch, but Pete wanted to stroll around Eastern Market. I inhaled a banana so we could meander through, stopping to pick up a card for my Dad's 60th birthday. At the card stand, Pete did something not cool, which he later agreed was not cool, and has since apologized. In the grand scheme of life, it was not that big of a deal but I absolutely *lost* it. I walked away in a semi-respectable fashion, but when we got back to the car I totally let him have it, screaming very loudly, in public, though I hope no one was paying attention. I was spitting mad, way madder than the incident deserved and the disproportionate nature of my anger made it all the more terrible. I even screamed and swore at him while he was wearing our precious baby. It was ugly, and by it, I mean, I. I was ugly.

I felt icky, and in the past, I would have dwelt on those feelings for days, avoiding my quiet times, beating myself up, and generally feeling like a failure. I know in my head that Jesus forgives us, and even before we sin, he has covered it. We are justified in God's eyes because he sees us through the eyes of Christ. It is finished.

But that principle doesn't always sit quite right with me. I also know that even though we are forgiven, there are still consequences for our sins. Sometimes we see and feel them, and sometimes we don't. In this instance, once Pete forgave me and I repented to the Lord, it didn't feel like anything was wrong anymore. Maybe there are consequences I can't see, like strangers or people I know judging my public meltdown (hopefully no one saw). Maybe Penny will have some weird latent memory of her parents fighting in front of her, or maybe she will learn swear words, (ahh I hope not!) but other than that, it was over. It felt too easy.

My friend Elaine is killing it in her career and I love hearing about her latest tips and strategies for success. A few years ago, she told me what they're teaching the world's best surgeons at Stanford: fail fast. Make a mistake, learn from it, and move on. It's a little disconcerting to think about heart surgeons "failing fast," but the concept is sound. Don't wallow, move past it.

In the spirit of failing fast, I decided to try accepting God's forgiveness at face value. As we shared a family walk in the afternoon, I chewed on it a little, seeing what it would feel like if I just believed it was OK, that God loved me, and had forgiven me as soon as I asked. I felt lighter. I felt free. And then I felt guilty for feeling lighter and free. I had just majorly sinned not five hours ago. What business did I have feeling light and free? So I listened to the lying voice of the enemy and said, "Nah, maybe not quite yet."

But what if it was over? What if we are supposed to walk in the truth of Psalm 103:10-12, "He does not treat us as our sins deserve or repay us according to our iniquities. For as high as the heavens are above the earth, so great is his love for those who fear him; as far as the east is from the west, so far has he removed our transgressions from us."

The next morning, this verse sealed the deal, "Here I am! I stand at the door and knock. If anyone hears my voice and opens the door, I will come in and eat with that person, and they with me" (Revelation 3:20). The Lord was knocking on my door, asking me to sit with him, to accept his grace. I opened the door and said yes.

Next time, when you're confronted by the ugliness of your own sin, don't let the enemy keep you from the presence of God. As fallible humans, the pattern of sin is inevitable. Like our laundry, we're on a continuous cycle of wash, rinse, repeat. Don't sit around in your dirty clothes when you're meant to be clothed in gleaming white. He has purchased you with his blood for this very purpose. "Cleanse me with hyssop, and I will be clean; wash me, and I will be whiter than snow" (Psalm 51:7).

Shorten the Cycle

But God demonstrates his own love for us in this: While we were still sinners, Christ died for us. (Romans 5:8)

[He] redeems your life from the pit, [he] crowns you with lovingkindness and compassion. (Psalm 103:4)

Unfortunately, I'm back to my old habits. I've been a bad actor. I took the bait, picked a fight, said mean things, and woke up feeling super crummy. Last night we had a big fight over nothing. You ladies know what I'm talking about, one of those fights when you're just cranky, irritable, and every little thing makes you mad. I'd like to say quinoa was the culprit, but quinoa was just the impetus, being an inoffensive protein-packed grain and all. I had made a huge batch of organic quinoa for us to eat throughout the week. While I was putting Penny to bed, Pete cleaned up the kitchen. He loathes quinoa but I keep trying to sneak it into everything because it's just so good for you and I'm determined to find a way to make him like it. I came downstairs to a clean kitchen but went apoplectic when I noticed the huge pile of quinoa in the trashcan. He had thrown away my whole big batch of quinoa and I was pretty mad about it.

We reconciled before bed because he apologized and I decided that quinoa wasn't worth going to sleep angry over, but when I woke up, I still had that lingering feeling of yuck. I'm increasingly more cognizant of the fact that when I blow it, I owe two apologies, two confessions, one to the person I hurt, and another to the Lord. It's funny how I'm eager to be restored to right relationship with the flesh and body people in my life, but I shy away from approaching God. I am ashamed, frustrated with myself, and feel undeserving of his presence and his grace. I skulk about, avoiding my Bible, until I've properly paid my penance or something. Then I begin the process of coming clean and restoring communication.

These one-sided estrangements used to last a lot longer, but over time, tenderly and persistently, the Lord is shortening the cycle. One day I hope to break the cycle altogether, but right now, I'll settle for shortening it. And that's exactly what God did for me this week. The very next morning, I prepared to feel like a big fat failure, rightly bowled over by reading some piercing, convicting scripture. But you know what I found instead? I found a God who sees me exactly as I am, who was drawing me back into sweet communion with him.

I read Romans 5:8 (RSV), "But God shows his love for us in that while we were yet sinners Christ died for us." Bam! It was clear, as if God himself was saying *directly to me*, "I see you, Natalie, I see your sin. I loved you when you were an unreconciled sinner and I love you now. Don't stay away from me, we have things to do together."

Because he wanted me to know that he sees me, he provided a much-needed word of exhortation from a caring friend. She kindly listened to me vent my frustration with my lack of self-control with my anger, and responded with this perfect, Holy Spirit insight:

> Sometimes it's the smallest things that set us off. It's just marriage. And our spouse is the only person who can make us madder than we ever think we can be. Even though they are the ones we love the

most. Satan is doing his very best to distract you, to
cause you to fixate. Tell him NO and try extra hard
to deflect his whispers.

She spoke the truth to me in love and I needed to hear it. The next day at Bible study, our leader mentioned a foothold concept I've found helpful over the years: when we find ourselves sliding down into the pit, whether the pit of anger, despair, self-pity, or envy, the Lord *always* provides a foothold to catch us on our descent. He provides something firm and immovable for us to grab onto, a grip to stay the downward spiral. This foothold might be a phrase of scripture to cling to, the encouraging words of a friend, or the voice of the Lord speaking to you through what you're already reading in your quiet time.

The more time I spend with the Lord, the more his Word springs readily to my mind and refutes the lying tongue of the enemy who wants to keep me from accessing grace. Gradually, I've found I slide a shorter distance into the pit rather than plummeting straight to the bottom. The cycles of separation produced by my sin are shortening. Shortening the cycle doesn't mean I'm forever off the hook for my bad behavior, or that I don't mourn the damage I've caused or the pain I've wrought.

Repentance is crucial; reconciliation is nonnegotiable, but wallowing in my guilt is optional. I'm learning to walk away from it. My Pursuer is calling me back, welcoming me into his presence, covering my shame with his grace.

The God of More Than Enough

Now to him who is able to do immeasurably more
than all we ask or imagine, according to his power
that is at work within us. (Ephesians 3:20)

It was I who taught Ephraim to walk, taking them by the arms;
but they did not realize it was I who healed them.
I led them with cords of human kindness, with ties of love.
To them I was like one who lifts a little child to the cheek,
and I bent down to feed them. (Hosea 11:3–4)

It's rainy outside and cozy inside. My baby is napping, I'm drinking chocolate chai tea, and our dog, Sam, is snuggled up next to me—one of those moments where all is well.

I'm reflecting on a conversation with a friend last week where she calmly remarked that her husband was in Asia for two weeks again, and I said, "Wow, how do you manage all his travel with your kids? Is it hard for you?"

She was quick to acknowledge the many challenges but was specific and clear in recounting how God has provided for them every time her husband travels.

He became the head of an international legal ministry five years ago. Before the Board offered him the role, they spent a long time interviewing her. They wanted to make sure she was comfortable with how much time it would require him to be away. She told them that had her kids been any younger, she wouldn't have been able to do it, but they were finally at the age where it could be manageable. As she relayed the story to me, she laughed as she said that the Lord confirmed it for them a zillion times. After much prayer and consideration, they accepted the position.

A few months passed, and her husband got ready for his first big international trip when he would be gone for two weeks. As the date drew closer, she found herself getting more and more anxious, thinking, "Ugh, what have I gotten myself into? How will I survive this? What did we sign up for?"

She mentally steeled herself to put her big girl panties on and "grin and bear it," powering her way through what was sure to be a long, lonely, and difficult couple of weeks. She kept asking the Lord, "Ok God, just help me *get through this.*" Just let it pass quickly.

But the Lord asked her, "Is that really what you think of me?" Do you really think that if I call your husband to a job that is wonderful and fulfilling for him, that there won't be enough left over for you? That I'm not capable of creating a situation where everyone thrives? A clear call from me does not immediately equal scarcity, lack, and hardship. Life with me is not a zero-sum game."

She repented of her attitude, saying, "Wow. Lord, you are a God of extravagant grace." He not only richly provided for their family during that trip, but has given her incredible grace over the last five years as her husband has continued to travel. Sure, it's an adjustment. Of course they miss him. But she said the only reason they can do it is because God has given them grace to accomplish that to which he has called them. And they are all thriving.

This story is a great reminder that life with God is not a zero sum game. We serve a God who can do immeasurably more than we can ask or imagine. Praise him for being a lavish God instead of a penny-pinching God. It's so much better to be the children of a generous Heavenly Father. When I find myself thinking, "I can't ask for that," or, "Of course, that's too good to be true," or, "I want that too much, it probably won't happen," I'm trying to catch myself. Instead, I take a moment to remember the occasions in my life and in others' lives where God has been lavish with us. I can choose to believe the goodness of his character or I can choose to believe he's out to get me. I am learning to choose to believe in his goodness.

In Hosea 11: 3–4, the imagery of God's love and guidance for Israel is profoundly tender. He leads us with "cords of human kindness, with ties of love." What does it mean to be led with cords of human kindness, with ties of love?

The Pulpit Commentary says this:

> Verse 4. I drew them with cords of a man, with bands of love … The **cords of a man** are such as parents use in leading weak or young children. **Bands of love** qualify more closely the preceding expression, "cords of a man," and are the opposite of those which men employ in taming or breaking wild and unmanageable animals … 'I have led Israel by the cords of a man, and not the cords of a heifer which one drags along with resistance, but as a man draws his fellow-man without compelling him to go with resistance: even so I have led them after a gentle method.[2]

He leads us so gently, drawing us near, like a parent delicately guiding a child just learning to walk. Penny's favorite thing to do right now is grasp our pointer fingers and walk down the stairs like a big girl or do laps around the house. I've got a gentle hold on her

---

[2]   Hosea 11:4. *The Pulpit Commentary*. *www.biblehub.com*. (Accessed March 25, 2015).

hands, and I whisper words of encouragement, "Good girl! You can do it! Keep going! What a big step!" She looks up at me, smiles, then keeps toddling forward in determination. We're a team, I'm leading her, but it's gentle and sweet, and every time we change direction it's to protect her, give her more space, or avoid a tricky obstacle. My whispered encouragement makes our "walks" a joyful, happy time together because she knows I am right there cheering her on, and she has back up whenever she needs it. That is how God leads us. He leads us with cords of love and kindness; he whispers encouragement in our ears; he plots the route for our benefit and our safety. Each step holding his hand signifies our continued desire to walk with him because his walk is the best walk you could ever imagine. His leading is an invitation, not a hard yank by the neck. Wherever he is leading you, rest assured that he will give you more than enough grace for the journey. He is the God of more than enough.

He Would Suffer, But He Would Win

For the joy set before him, he endured the cross,
scorning its shame, and sat down at the right hand
at the throne of God. (Hebrews 12:2)

Today, I am tired. I recognize it as a kind of soul tired. It's been several days since I spent some good time with the Lord and I miss it. I need it. I get overwhelmed, irritable, and I lose my *joie de vivre* when I don't regularly spend time with the Lord. He is our *daily* bread, not our *once or twice a week after the laundry is folded and dinner is prepped and if Penny naps long enough* bread. During her second (and hopefully longer!) nap, I finally had a chance to sit down with the Lord.

In *Live a Praying Life*®, the author, Jennifer Kennedy Dean, explores the characteristics of living a praying life and offers profound insight on suffering and prayer. I have the anniversary edition of the study and the author has made quite a few notes and added appendices since she lost her husband to brain cancer in 2005. Her understanding of prayer and God's purposes in allowing suffering has deepened since enduring that experience.

Personally, I fear suffering. I fear interruptions. I hate that the things and people I cherish cannot remain static. People I love are aging, my sweet baby is growing up in front of my eyes, and this delightful season we're in cannot and will not last forever. I wish I wouldn't waste a moment of my happy time feeling anxious about when or if everything will change, but that's a discipline I've not yet mastered. I'm constantly dodging the fear that the other shoe is going to drop. My sunny days are marred by fictitious clouds on the horizons, taunting me with the oldest of lies, "Nothing good will ever last. Things have been too good for you; it's all about to go up in flames." It's not a complete lie. My happy circumstances will probably change. Not every day of my life will be (or has been) daisies, buttercups, and roses. But that doesn't mean it won't be good.

What I'm learning to discern is that God's pruning is a skillful work of love. The pain I experience is but a shadow of what I deserve, and the new growth experienced through his grace is his kindness to me. (Even as I write this, I'm nervous. Am I taunting the enemy to have a go at me? Am I saying, "Hey! Over here, Lord, I could use a good clipping!") No, God isn't sitting up in heaven thinking, "Whoops, things have been good for Natalie for a little too long, better drop that other shoe, which one should we use to crush her?" That punishing image of God is utterly contrary to his character as proved over and over in scripture. God is merciful, he is kind, he loves to give us good gifts, but we hold this in tension with the fact that he does allow suffering.

Here's an illuminating excerpt from *Live a Praying Life*®:

> I think it is easier to tell people that we can avoid suffering and be protected from all pain than it is to tell people that pain is unavoidable and is to be embraced for the work it will do in our lives. We have this mentality that says that every bad thing that happens is Satan attacking. Maybe it is God's

pruning. Isn't it interesting that the branch bearing much fruit gets not protected, not babied, not put in a dust-proof display cabinet for all to admire, but pruned. Cut back. Injured. And why? So that it can bear more fruit.

If we cherish our comfort and value our status quo, then we can never let pain in to do its transforming work. If we resent the intrusion of the crucifixion, then we will never experience the wonder of resurrection. At some point in the very depths of my grief, I asked the Lord, "If You bear my burdens, then why do I have to feel this pain?" …

The Lord seemed to say to me: I stand between you and any blows headed your way. The blows meant for you land on Me. If the pain you feel hurts, just imagine the blow I absorbed for you. It should have been a knockout punch, but you will never feel the full force of a blow. A praying life—a life lived in the flow of His power and provision—does not promise life without pain. It promises life without knockout punches.[3]

A life without knockout punches. What a gift from God! He protects us from the things that are meant to bowl us over. He prunes us so that we can bear his fruit.

This morning, snuggled in our tufted, adorable, and woefully uncomfortable rocker, Penny and I were reading the story of Jesus' temptation in the desert in *The Jesus Storybook Bible*. The

[3] Dean, Jennifer Kennedy. *Live a Praying Life*. Anniversary Edition. ©2010 Jennifer Kennedy Dean *Live a Praying Life*® is published by New Hope Publishers. All Rights Reserved.

language in a children's version of a Bible story is so forthright and straightforward that it often gets the point across in a whole new way. At the end of the story, the author recounts how Jesus chose to be obedient to God even though it would mean enduring pain, saying, "He would suffer, but he would win."[4] Christ suffered for us, but the wonderful, life-changing truth is that he wins! He endured scars, suffering, and pain so that we could win through him and be redeemed. Though we may endure pain on this side of eternity, Christ's once-and-for-all sacrifice for our sins protects us from knockout punches and secures for us a place in heaven, that we may dwell forever in his glorious presence. Hallelujah!

---

4   Lloyd-Jones, Sally. *The Jesus Storybook Bible*. Grand Rapids: Zondervan, 2007.

Refined Like Gold

Though there are no sheep in the pen and no cattle in the stalls, yet I will rejoice in the Lord, I will be joyful in God my Savior. (Habakkuk 3:17–18)

Rejoice always, pray continually, give thanks in all circumstances for this is God's will for you in Christ Jesus. (1 Thessalonians 5:16–18)

It's Thanksgiving, a time for celebration and gratitude, yet the concept of adversity, and specifically *thanksgiving* in adversity has been showing up everywhere in my life this week. When the Lord keeps bringing the same concept up, it's wise to pay attention.

Our sermon on Sunday was about the purposes and importance of adversity, and how it is actually appropriate to contemplate adversity as we head into Thanksgiving. The theme of adversity came up again at my law firm's weekly devotional lunch. I work at a firm filled with incredibly kind, godly, and brilliant attorneys who serve their clients well. These attorneys also know how to exercise great discretion, such as remaining silent when I started wearing my black "dress" Uggs to work every day while seven months pregnant. They also pretended it was completely normal for me to move my "office" to the firm's massage chair all day when I was nine months pregnant, bless them.

At our weekly devotional lunch, one of the attorneys shared about giving thanks in adversity and why it's so good for us. To illustrate, she showed us a steel manufacturing plant she used to visit right in the middle of Chicago. The pictures revealed the incredible and surprisingly beautiful process of melting, refining, and re-melting required to strengthen the steel.

She made the important distinction that some adversity causes us to identify sin and repent, clearing away the dross. But other adversity is not necessarily related to sin. For example, the refining process to create gold involves melting and purifying the gold over and over again. The first time, the gold is melted and purified to remove impurities. Then the process becomes about strengthening and hardening the gold, making it purer, more beautiful, and durable. Adversity can be used by God not only to identify areas of sin and the need for repentance, but also to take us from 10 karat, to 14 karat, to 24 karat gold. He can use adversity to make us pure and beautiful and strong.

This guy I used to work for always said, "you can't polish a turd." And it's true. Some things that happen are just horrible, ugly, and evil. But we serve a God who is the redeemer of all things, who specializes in turning the ugly into the beautiful, and asking us to grow and have faith when it's painful, raw, and confusing.

A few days later, I came across a devotional referencing Habakkuk 3:17–18, a passage in which Habakkuk chooses, as a matter of will and obedience, to "rejoice in the Lord," and to "be joyful in God my Savior." Even though the fig trees do not bud and there are no sheep in the pen, Habakkuk gives thanks and praise to God. What if we, like Habakkuk, decided to give thanks in the midst of adversity? What if we started looking for how God meets us in the darkness instead of solely offering thanks for the light?

This morning, I wrote out a list of all the things that caused me hurt in this past year. I recorded the pain, difficulties, disappointments, and frustrations, especially those moments when I've felt like a failure. Next, I wrote in my journal, "Lord, I thank you for walking with me in this, I praise you for loving me. I thank you for making my eternal home secure." It's a challenging exercise, to look at all your hurts over the past year and choose to praise God for his unfailing love and faithfulness. I don't think my head and my heart are completely aligned on the practice of "giving thanks in all circumstances," but Scripture is unequivocally clear on this point. We are supposed to give thanks in all circumstances, even when everything is in shambles (or to quote my friend Jordon a hot mess dumpster fire).

God knows a thing or two about human nature, so it makes sense that he would ask us to praise him in adversity. As humans, we are weak and frail, perpetually seeking pleasure, comfort, and relief. Yet challenges make us grow. Challenges increase our faith, giving us an awareness of our need for God. God knows we are weak, so he gives us the antidote to becoming discouraged in the midst of adversity. He exhorts us to "rejoice always, pray continually, and give thanks without ceasing," setting our eyes upon him, the "author and perfecter of our faith" (1 Thessalonians 5:16–18)(Hebrews 12:2). Psalm 16 captures this exactly, "I have set the Lord always before me, because he is at my right hand, I will not be shaken" (Psalm 16:8 ESV). If we set the Lord always before us, our focus is on him, not on our circumstances. When we gaze upon his beauty and his goodness, contemplating our eternal place at his side, our circumstances often fade into the background.

If you're in the thick of it, rejoicing always and praying continually may feel wholly foreign, unnatural even. Still, we serve a God who doesn't follow the playbook of the world. "For my thoughts are not your thoughts, neither are your ways my ways" (Isaiah 55:8). He tells us plainly that he has a different plan for his people, a distinctive way of being, characterized by peace. John 14:27 says, "Peace I leave with you; my peace I give you. I do not give to you as the world gives. Do not let your hearts be troubled and do not be afraid." When he tells us to rejoice always, pray continually, and give thanks without ceasing, he is offering us his peace in the midst of struggle. He's saying, "This is the last thing you're going to feel like doing, but trust me, it will be your saving grace." My prayer for you is that as you experience adversity, you would not be overcome. May you choose to let him refine you, making you pure, durable, and strong.

The Pursuer

> Then you will call upon me and come and pray to me and I will listen to you. You will seek me and find me when you seek me with all your heart. I will be found by you, declares the Lord, and will bring you back from captivity. (Jeremiah 29:12–14a)

We're getting ready for a snow day tomorrow. We hit the store, which was complete chaos. Not a can of beans was to be found—apparently everyone in DC decided that a blizzard is the perfect time to make chili. There's hardly a roll of toilet paper or a bottle of water to be found in the entire city, and the beer stock was also looking pretty depleted. Snow, chili, and beer—can't go wrong with those three. We're finally home and ready to hunker down, help captive inside by the weather.

On my slow journey through the Bible, I'm currently reading Jeremiah, a book depicting a very different kind of captivity than the cozy closeting mandated by a blizzard. I'm not going to lie, Jeremiah has been rough for me. There's so much sin, judgment, and destruction that I finally had to add in a Psalm a day because I was a little bummed out and kind of forgetting about God's goodness. Amidst the turmoil, there are some beautiful, hopeful parts in the book of Jeremiah. The glory of God's grace and the magnificence of his redemption and sacrifice wouldn't mean as much if they weren't so distinctly contrasted with our sin, our deaf ears, our black hearts, and our utter depravity.

Jeremiah 29 contains a verse you may know and love, "For I know the plans I have for you," declares the Lord, "plans to prosper you and not to harm you, plans to give you hope and a future" (Jeremiah 29:11). This verse provides wonderful encouragement and we would all do well to learn it and pray it frequently. Yet any verse plucked from its surroundings can lose some of the richness of its meaning if it doesn't have the context in which it was originally given.

In Jeremiah 29, God speaks. I *love* the chapters in the Bible where the Lord speaks. For example, I always cry when reading the very end of Job, when there's been so much speculating by Job and all his "wise" friends, but at the end, the Lord speaks. His words are majestic and moving and so much better than all the paltry earthly wisdom Job and his friends offered up in the preceding chapters.

Jeremiah 29 is a letter to the exiles in Babylon. Basically everyone in Israel screwed up really bad and the whole country was destroyed. The super wicked Israelites perished in Israel, but the Lord preserved a small remnant that was taken into exile in Babylon for 70 years. In chapter 29, God tells the remnant what to do while they're in exile, "build houses, marry, have children, pray for the peace of the city in which you live, etc."

In verses 10–14, God says this:

> When seventy years are completed for Babylon, I will come to you and fulfill my gracious promise to bring you back to this place. For I know the plans I have for you, declares the Lord, "plans to prosper you and not to harm you, plans to give you hope and a future. Then you will call upon me and come and pray to me and I will listen to you. You will

seek me and find me when you seek me with all your heart. I will be found by you," declares the Lord, "and will bring you back from captivity. I will gather you from all the nations and places where I have banished you," declares the Lord, "and will bring you back to the place from which I carried you into exile."

Let's start at the beginning of verse 10. First of all, the Jews have to do their time. They have to pay penance for their great sin. The takeaway is that we serve a very gracious God, but that doesn't mean that the consequences of our sin disappear. The condemnation is covered in Christ, but sometimes the consequences, real and painful, remain, and we must accept them. Next God says I will, "fulfill my gracious promise to bring you back."

He is (1) a gracious God and (2) a God who keeps his promises and does what he says he's going to do when he says he's going to do it. He has plans for us. Really, really good plans, not the kind of scary, I'm worried God is out to get me kind of plans. Or the being a good Christian will mean everything in my life is always hard and terrible kind of plans. Good plans. Sometimes I struggle with believing in a good and gracious God, so this part is especially important for me. God knows our future. His plans are good and full of hope. We may experience pain and trials, but the Lord our God goes with us and gives us hope.

Early in our marriage, Pete and I were working through some challenging issues. I vividly recall being on the phone with my Dad, sitting on the curb in front of a swanky craft coffee store and crying my eyes out. My Dad said, "Natalie, this is difficult, but you don't have to be afraid of the outcome or the struggle. Imagine you're playing a game but you already know who wins. When you look up at the scoreboard, you have already won in Christ. The outcome is certain and secure." That is gospel truth right there. We have already won in Christ. Therefore, we *have hope.*

We have a gracious God, with good plans, who gives us a hope and a future. So what's next?

God says his people will call upon him, come to him, and pray to him ... and then he will listen. He promises to listen to our prayers and to receive us when we come to him. In verse 13, he promises something radical, "when you seek me you *will* find me, when you seek me with all your heart. I will *be found by you and bring you back from captivity.*"

Let's talk about all the amazing promises in this brief passage. When we show up to meet with God, we will always find him. I often experience God in small glimmers, or in one little corner of my life. But I long to dwell in his presence. That's why I love the promise of this verse, "When you look for me, I'll be there." Plain and simple. Perhaps my problem is the way I'm looking, or the fact that I'm not looking for him very much or very diligently. Whatever my shortcomings, he promises to be found when I seek him.

I love the phrase at the end of verse 14, "I will be found by you." God is reiterating the same point, "when you seek me you will find me," and then again, "I will be found be you," just in case we didn't get it the first time. Maybe our brains are helped a bit when he switches the words around for us. Lastly, the kicker, "[I will] bring you back from captivity," which symbolizes our great freedom. Through the restoration of his rescue, we are free from slavery to sin. We are made new through the sacrifice of Christ. We don't have to live in the bondage where the enemy wants to keep us. God is bringing us back from captivity, into the place he has prepared for us, and to the "plans he has for us."

The phrase, "I will bring you back from captivity," brings to mind a conversation with a friend about the ubiquity of the strong, pursuing, and often-controlling male character portrayed in novels and films. Women are eating up this genre of male pursuit like ice cream and candy. America is eating it up. We are hungry for more; we are hungry to be pursued.

My friend observed that this type of media appeals to the deep longing many women have to be pursued, sought after, known, loved, and cherished by a man with a plan. In the face of a million decisions, the idea of man who always knows exactly what to do and how to do it is intoxicating. We are entranced by archetypal romantic characters, but they are not rooted in reality. Yet their essence appeals to something elemental and deep within us.

It's natural to long for a hero to arrive with unconditional love and all the answers, protections, and provisions you will ever need. This longing is representative of the God-shaped hole we each have in our hearts. We were created to yearn for God in the deepest place of our souls. We were made to trust him, and to be intimately acquainted with him. He is the *only one* who can be our archetypal hero. He is the *only one* who will pursue us relentlessly, love us perfectly, and cherish us poignantly. Our novels and films try, and usually fail, to capture that eternal romance we can only experience through relationship with our Creator.

God is the ultimate pursuer. He always has a plan. He is always working things together for our good. We can rest in his arms, assured that he will *bring us back from captivity*.

Rest in the knowledge that he has a plan. His heart is to bring you back from captivity if you'll let him.

While lying awake at 4:30 a.m. on Wednesday morning, I was thinking about other verses in Scripture that outline God's pursuing heart toward us. Psalms and Proverbs are full of rich imagery describing the way God pursues us, rescues us, and protects us. Proverbs 18:10, "The name of the Lord is a strong tower, the righteous run into it and are safe," and Psalm 139:7–8, "Where can I go from your Spirit? Where can I flee from your presence? If I go up to the heavens, you are there; if I make my bed in the depths, you are there," both speak of God's constant protection, presence, and pursuit.

Scripture is also full of exhortations to follow hard after God. One of my favorites is Isaiah 62:6, "You who call on the Lord, give yourselves no rest." It's a peculiar phrase but creates a striking picture. What if we gave ourselves no rest in calling on the Lord? What if we started pursuing God as he pursues us? In our prayers, our worship, our adoration, and our petitioning, we are called to give him no rest. It's not just an invitation to appeal to our Heavenly Father; it's a simple but compellingly-worded command. When we call on the name of the Lord without rest, we will not be disappointed. Our quest for God is not one-sided, as we pursue him, we are pursuing the ultimate Pursuer. There is always reciprocity in our pursuit of God. In fact, we can only even begin to pursue him because he first loved us (1 John 4:19). Don't give up. Press in. Persist and persevere. Give him no rest!

Jesus: Our Great Intercessor

> My heart is steadfast, O God; I will sing and make
> music with all my soul. (Psalm 108:1)

I love the complete confidence with which the psalmist writes in Psalm 108. My heart is steadfast, O God; I will sing and make music with all my soul. The language is simple, yet proclaims that his heart *is steadfast.* It's not, "Lord, make me steadfast," or "Oh, I wish I were steadfast." He simply states, "My heart is steadfast, O God."

Next week, I'm heading into a day of meetings with congressional staffers and I need to be steadfast. I need to praise God *with all my soul.* I always get a little nervous/excited before a big day of meetings. It feels a bit like doing battle (in a good way). I try to spend more time with the Lord on those days because (a) I have a short commute and (b) I know I need it. I need to be grounded in the Word so I can deal with whatever is going on in my heart, making way for the Holy Spirit to equip me for the day's work. I need to be reminded that God very clearly gave me this job, thus I can confidently ask him for the skill and ability to do it well. I also like to put on my physical "armor" for big meetings—the killer shoes my husband gave me one year for Christmas, the special pendant my parents gave me as a graduation gift, and a big-girl pencil skirt.

In my read-through-the-Bible nonplan, I had almost finished with the gospels, and while I was eager to read through the rest of the New Testament with fresh eyes, I was also a little sad to leave the flesh and blood Jesus behind. In John 17, I was gobsmacked by Jesus' prayer for the disciples in verses 6–19:

> I have revealed you to those *whom you gave me out of the world*. They were yours; you gave them to me and they have obeyed your word. Now they know that everything you have given me comes from you. For I gave them the words you gave me and they accepted them. They knew with certainty that I came from you, and they believed that you sent me. *I pray for them*. I will remain in the world no longer, but they are still in the world, and I am coming to you. *Holy Father, protect them by the power of your name—the name you gave me—so that they may be one as we are one … My prayer is not that you would take them out of the world but that you protect them from the evil one. They are not of the world, even as I am not of it. Sanctify them by the truth; your word is truth. As you sent me into the world, I have sent them into the world. For them I sanctify myself, that they too may be truly sanctified* (emphasis mine).

This passage is chock full of incredible spiritual truths, but here are a few (ok, five) observations. First, we, as believers, have been <u>given by God to Jesus out of the world</u>. Even though we may be physically in the world, our relationship to the world is fundamentally altered by the power of our redemption through Christ. You cannot give what you do not own. In order for God to give us <u>out of the world</u>, we must first submit to God's ownership of our lives. Once we accept his ownership, our spiritual address changes. We are owned by God, redeemed by Christ, and set apart for his purposes. This is how we may be in the world but not of it.

Second, <u>Jesus prays for us</u> (I pray for them)! This phrase is not in the past tense, but in the present tense. He prays for us continually at the right hand of God. This conjures up the image of Aslan, the mighty, wondrous, and wise lion representing Jesus in the *Chronicles of Narnia*, interceding for me. If you've never read the *Chronicles of Narnia*, buy them, read them, cherish them. If you read *The Chronicles of Narnia* as a child, reread them. We definitely want Aslan on our prayer team.

Third, in his prayers for us, <u>Jesus asks for protection from the evil one</u>. He covers us with his prayers. He asks that our thoughts, physical bodies, relationships, and families would be protected from Satan. The fact that Jesus prays this way demonstrates the protection and power we have in our relationship with him, but also reminds us that evil is a real and persistent presence in the world. We must not ignore the need to ask for protection. We must be on alert, even as we go about seemingly mundane tasks.

Fourth, his prayer for us is <u>not that God would call us out of the world</u>, thus we are supposed to be here. We are meant to be in the world, working out our sanctification, glorifying him with our lives, and winning others to salvation by living as the aroma of Christ.

Fifth and finally, we are sanctified (the lifelong process of being made perfect in Christ) by the truth (<u>sanctify them by your truth</u>). We are made perfect through, grow in, and are nourished by the truth. Where is this wonderfully curative truth? Boom: *your word is truth* (v. 17). The Word of God is truth. We need the Word of the Lord in us as truth to experience sanctification. The Bible is very important for every single thing, all the time, no ifs, ands, or buts!

Jesus, in his great grace and lovingkindness towards us, prays for us continually. He asks his Heavenly Father on our behalf. It's much easier to face a big scary day at work when you know that *Jesus himself* is praying for you! Be encouraged to pray for strength to do the work he has for you, knowing that Jesus is and forever will be interceding for you!

Take Root.

Two Fists

May my prayer be set before you like incense; may the lifting up of my hands be like the evening sacrifice. (Psalm 141:2)

We finally arrived back in DC after celebrating Christmas in California with my family. Surviving that cross-country flight felt like finishing a marathon and I am *so* relieved to be done. Traveling with babies is not for the faint of heart. And we were lucky! On both legs, we had a row to ourselves, which felt like (scratch that, *was*) an answer to prayer. The first night back, I sat on my couch in the dark with my Christmas jammies on, wearing my sleep mask on my forehead, a half a Tylenol PM in my system but still wide awake. Thank you, time change.

In my time-change-induced insomnia, I spent time reflecting on that funny time of year where Christmas is behind us but it's not quite the new year with its fresh slate and hopeful resolve. This span of five or six days usually involves travel and goodbyes, which I'm never fond of, but I also find it to be an excellent time for reflection.

This particular season, I reflected on the relational dynamics surrounding holidays. They're joyous and celebratory, but also bear the weight of so many people's expectations. This can lead to conflict, dissatisfaction, and offenses that build up over the years. The "she always says thats," and the "why do they always do thats" abound. No matter how blissful your family life, difficult situations come up, and in any case, difficult people will always exist.

This Christmas I did a lot of observing—conversations, relationships, group dynamics, watching the give-and-take of making a holiday come together.

When you grow up and get married, holidays change. It's tough for everyone. 99.9% of the time, I *love* that I now have two families who love me, and that my brother has two families who love him. Yet when Christmas rolls around, I desperately want all of us to have clones and be in two places at once. One family's joyous year together brings another family's sadness with empty seats around the table. It hurts when the traditions you hold sacred and dear change even when it's for the best. It makes me long for my simple childhood when my brother and I would wake up in the middle of the night and sneak downstairs to look at the presents and enjoy the magic of the Christmas tree lit in the quiet darkness. Now we're older; he lives nearby and doesn't stay at my parents' house on Christmas Eve. We live in DC and alternate holidays between our two families. I miss those times together. But we've all figured out a schedule that works for everyone, each of us doing our best to spend as much time as we can together and make everybody feel loved. It's the way of life, to grow up. Our families expand and are richer because of it. But still, it means change and change always hurts a little.

We had a wonderful time together this Christmas, but we still had a few *moments*. Even in the loveliest of families who sing carols around the Christmas tree, drink cocoa, and share deep, meaningful thoughts on Advent and the Incarnation, there are *moments*. You know what I mean by *moments*—those things that make your blood boil, or make you feel like you've just been sucker punched, or are just plain irritating. So that's why my mom and I decided that our two fists could help us navigate these *moments*.

When you go through the whole effort to get your baby out the door for the Christmas Eve service and there are no seats in either service location (and your hair is wet and you run into at least 4 people you haven't seen in 10 years, awesome), don't fret. When your baby is crying and throwing an ungodly amount of food on the floor in a nice restaurant, don't be dismayed. When someone flippantly dismisses your hard work and effort, or worse, doesn't acknowledge it, don't immediately take offense. Instead, here's our game plan: I want you to ball up your two fists, but not to throw a punch. You're going to tap into the grace of our Heavenly Father.

Do you have your two fists ready?

We're clutching our right hand tightly shut and we begin to pray. Even if it's breathless and broken, start praying. In our right hand, we lay down whatever or whoever is making us sad or angry, and gradually, our tight fist loosens. Imagine your prayer rising to the throne room of heaven and away from your clutching grip. You're freer, lighter. (Note: the things that flare up might be a single incident in a series of wounds and hurts, and there might be more to pray into later, but this will help you keep your stuff together through dinner.)

Psalm 141:2 says, "May my prayer be set before you like incense; may the lifting up of my hands be like the evening sacrifice." Our prayers are delightful incense before the Lord, even our desperate, hurried prayers are a sacrifice to him.

Revelation 5:8 says, "And when he had taken it, the four living creatures and the twenty-four elders fell down before the Lamb. Each one had a harp and they were holding golden bowls full of incense, which are the prayers of God's people." I am not going to pretend to exegete what is going on in the rest of that verse, but here's what we do know: our prayers are held in golden bowls as incense to be presented before the Heavenly Father. He is delighted when we acknowledge our need for and reliance on him through our prayers. This pleases him just like the scent of browned-butter-sea-salt-nutella-stuffed chocolate chip cookies pleases any human alive ever.

In your right hand, you have prayer. In your left hand, you have gratitude. Balling up your left fist, start to make a list of the things you're grateful for, starting with the person or situation that's pushing your button. Maybe it's only, "at least I have a family to get on my nerves and I'm not alone," or "at least we care enough to engage," or "at least we're still communicating." Or maybe this brief exercise is enough to jolt you out of the tiny thing that was throwing you off kilter, giving you a chance to look up and survey the beauty around you. The people you *love* are gathered, this is your *family*, and most importantly, we come together (at Christmas) because *God decided to redeem us!* One by one, the fingers on your left hand will uncurl.

In your two fists you now have prayer and gratitude. Prayer releases whatever we need to let go of and gratitude gives us perspective. This year my grandmother gave each of us a beautiful and thoughtful gratitude journal to encourage us to write down our grateful lists. I know gratitude is having a moment, but isn't that marvelous? One of the most profound tools we can use to combat the work of the enemy, and keep ourselves focused on God, is having a heyday in our secular culture. I love it when God's truth comes at us from every angle. Give this exercise a shot. It works, I promise.

Once the moment is past, it's time for a little introspection, a little analysis of the common thread. This common thread idea came up in a conversation I had with a family member about dealing with difficult people. She's had her fair share of difficult people to deal with, and she shared some handy tips for how to cope. For instance, if someone reads her the riot act, here's what she does: she listens to what they have to say, then she brings it before the Lord and asks the Holy Spirit to help her determine what she needs to repent of (where she's wrong, and what she needs to work on), and then she asks the Lord to take away the rest of it.

Psalm 139:23–24 says, "Search me, O God, and know my heart; test me and know my anxious thoughts. See if there is any offensive way in me, and lead me in the way everlasting." As David writes, we are to ask the Lord to sift our spirit, to weigh our character. As the Holy Spirit convicts, he will gently work with us on those areas of sin, and we can confidently let the rest fall away.

One of the most helpful things anyone has ever said to me was, "Natalie, be a duck, be a duck, be a duck." What do ducks do? They let the water roll right off their backs. Their feathers are designed to repel water, keeping them toasty and warm even as they swim in frigid waters.

Oh, that we would all be like ducks! Whatever junk doesn't belong to us, whatever freezing water the enemy wants to use against us, may it roll off our backs like a duck. After our conversation, I started thinking about the part where you ask the Lord to show you where to repent. It got me thinking, we all have difficult people in our lives, but what's the only thing they all have in common? Us. That's right, we're the common thread.

Now, I'm not saying other people aren't mean, or rude, or crazy. They're probably all three. But we can't control them. The only person you have control over is yourself. And by control, I mean the ability to lay the situation before the foot of the cross. The only and best recourse we have is to ask the Lord where we can grow in those relationships, ask him to show us where we need to repent, how we need to think or act or speak differently, and then ask for the supernatural power of the Holy Spirit so we can *do it*.

You might find the Lord gives you compassion and empathy for this person. You might find he gives you grace. You might find that what you really thought was another person's problem is your own stuff he wants to gently remove. The possibilities are endless! As these situations arise, and they will come, I encourage you to think about the common thread, ask Jesus to show you what you need to keep and sort through, and let the rest roll off your back like a duck. Use prayer and gratitude to keep your sanity!

Unscheduled Saturdays

When my spirit grows faint within me, it is you who know my way. (Psalm 142:3)

I have been so tired lately. There are decisions that need to be made, things that need doing, and I don't have any socks or underwear because I haven't done laundry in two weeks. I also don't have any deodorant because the internet lied about 2-day shipping.

Because we've been so tired, we implemented a new rest technique around here and it's going well. I am a person who wants to say yes to everything. I want to make new friends and include new people, along with growing existing relationships with friends all over the world. As I'm struggling to learn, we have a finite amount of time and a finite amount of energy. My husband is a total introvert. He loves hunting (being alone in the woods), fishing (being alone in a stream), biking (being alone on a trail), and hiking (being alone in the wilderness). Are you catching a theme here? This guy needs some alone time to be a functioning human.

This trait completely mystified me when we first got married. He would walk in the door and I would say, "Hi!! How are you? How was your day? What did you do? Who did you talk to? What did you have for lunch? What do you want for dinner? Do you want a beer or a gin and tonic?" All this before he even took off his tie. Needless to say, our first year of marriage was an adjustment period. I learned to give him some space right when he walks in the door. Now that we have a child, it's harder for me to give him a few minutes to unwind, but we try to strike a balance.

My sweet, introverted husband has helped me realize the importance of dedicated rest. Because we both read *The Rest of God* by Mark Buchanan early in our relationship, we have always been pretty diligent about Sabbath. In addition to Sabbath rest, we are exploring a different kind of rest, and it's all about being *unscheduled*. He told me he needs a 24-hour period once a week that is unscheduled in order to rest. Since Saturday is the most restful day of the weekend, we shoot for unscheduled Saturdays. I confess I'm not great at it. I want to see people, do things, and accept invitations. Plus, so many fun things happen on Saturdays! Nevertheless, we're trying as hard as we can to have one day, 24 hours each week, to be unscheduled and do whatever we feel like doing. This doesn't always happen, but even the idea of it makes us feel better. The benefits of deliberately creating time and space to rest have lent a calmer, less chaotic cadence to our busy weekdays.

I used to think that an empty calendar meant I had to say yes to every opportunity that came my way. Now I'm learning that we can "schedule" our time to be unscheduled. We can be free to say we have plans because we do, with ourselves. The fruit of this rest has been remarkable in our marriage and family life. We are more connected, more relaxed, and far less stressed when we honor the Sabbath. Life doesn't stretch on like an endless busy marathon, but instead becomes punctuated by sustaining rest, just as God intended. I'm also learning that giving my husband the space and time to breathe and feel human means we get the very best of him throughout the week.

As an enthusiastic extrovert, I am learning that I really do enjoy a slower pace and free time to be spontaneous or relax. Is there a better feeling than waking up on a Saturday and seeing nothing on the horizon but a free day to hold adventure, rest, and quality time? It's pure bliss. Our most recent unscheduled Saturday included a delicious of morning of sleeping in for me (yes!), a family walk through a new area of DC, and a little trek down the C&O trail to see the birds along the Potomac River. Pete cooked lunch, we played with Penny, watched a movie, and went to bed early. Seriously, it was a perfect day!

If you're not currently observing the Sabbath, start working it into your life. Take one day or even a half-day a week to rest and enjoy God's beautiful world. Do it. I promise, it's the best. I observed Sabbath all through law school, *even while studying for the bar exam.* If it feels overwhelming to think of making space for a whole day of rest, just remember that God *created you for Sabbath.* He modeled it for us by observing Sabbath himself. Like yeast leavens dough, Sabbath touches every corner of life, refreshing, invigorating, and nourishing our spirits. If you're already rocking Sabbath, spend some time thinking about what feels restful to you and your family. Sabbath Saturdays are restful for our family and we try to honor that time. Think about how you can incorporate restfulness into your days and weeks. Take time to refocus, to rest, and worship. Most of all, enjoy yourself!

Boundary Lines in Pleasant Places

Lord, you have assigned me my portion and my cup;
you have made my lot secure.
The boundary lines have fallen for me in pleasant places;
Surely I have a delightful inheritance. (Psalm 16:5–6)

I'm finally feeling rested for the first time since the beginning
of December, which seems like a very long time ago. With travel,
teething, and sickness, it's been a while since we've slept through
the night and I feel gloriously human again. The last two nights,
Pete and I have been fighting off a little flu bug by getting in bed
by 7:00 p.m. Yep, that's right, 7:00 p.m. We put Penny to bed, and
then follow suit. It. Is. Amazing. Unfortunately, we had to bail on a
dinner with neighbors, but still it was an excellent decision. I said
I would bring a meal over to their house, so I delivered the dinner
and then hightailed it home to be in my bed by 7:00 p.m. (Can I say
7:00 p.m. enough times?!)

This new year I've been thinking about what I'd like life to look
like, and then in discouragement, remember that I seem to have
very little control over anything because I have a baby. That's not
the whole truth. I can always work on my attitude. I can adopt a
few guiding principles to inform my decision-making over the next

few months. Resolutions are off the table, it's too strong a word for me right now. Do I wish I were getting up at 5:30 a.m. to alternate between the 6:00 a.m. spin class or an inspired morning quiet time every day of the week? Yes, I do. But let's be real, that's not going to happen. So why don't I start thinking about things that I can do that won't pile mounds of guilt on top of this already guilt-prone conscience? Thus, guiding principles it is.

Guiding Principle #1: Make Fewer Plans Far In Advance

I've said this guiding principle out loud a few times now, and each time I do, it feels a little less scary. Washington, DC is one of the most over-scheduled cities in the world. People plan their lives so far in advance it's crazy. I grew up in a family of planners; I am a planner. Because I'm a pre-processor, I like to anticipate all the fun things coming up ahead. I like to anticipate what it's going to be like, how I'm going to feel, what we'll do, see, talk about, and eat. Pre-planning isn't a bad thing. It just doesn't work well for us right now.

Over the last few months, I've noticed that whenever I make plans far in advance, even good plans that are not supposed to be stressful, it almost always blows up in my face. Host homegroup once a month? Sure, not a big deal! Yet when that Thursday comes around, I'm frantically trying to clean my house with a cranky baby, Pete ends up having to work late, and I find myself with someone knocking on my door fifteen minutes before homegroup starts while I'm nursing and trying to put Penny to bed. (Please, if you love me, do not arrive at my house early.)

It's virtually impossible to live life without making plans. Nevertheless, I am starting to implement this principle to set a boundary line whenever I can. Every time I do, it feels like a huge weight has been lifted off my shoulders. For instance, every time I find myself about to say, "Come over for dinner next Friday," I pause and tell myself, "Wait, Natalie. You have no idea what the next

10 days will hold, so you can wait a little to make plans." Making fewer plans far in advance is a little recalibration for us to figure out how to stay sane. The flip side is that we will be available for more impromptu hangouts! We had a beautiful impromptu hangout on Sunday with dear friends and it was splendid. In reality, the person most affected by this principle is me. I like to initiate and plan and set dates, just not in this season of life.

You may be in a completely opposite season. You might be adding structure, plans, routine, discipline—whatever you need to stay sane, and that's awesome. You might be like my sister-in-law, who has more self-control and discipline than anyone else I know, and eschew New Year's resolutions altogether. Someday, I hope to be like that. Wouldn't it be great to wake up on January 1st and say, "Hey, we've got a pretty good thing going here, let's not shake it up this year?" Wherever you are, I want to encourage you to listen to the Lord about where your boundary lines need to be. If you've got a rhythm, keep it up. If you need to make some changes, be honest with yourself and persevere.

Guiding Principle #2: If it's Not a YES, Then It's a NO

This principle is blatantly stolen from my friend Mae. I have to be honest that it feels ridiculous coming from me, but at least she knows I'm riffing off her thoughtful inspiration, so we're good.

A few days ago, as she was wisely text-advising me on all things motherhood, she shared this fabulous quote from Jen Hatmaker's Instagram, and I've decided to adopt this as my filter for the year:

> [T]hat medium yes, that I-feel-like-I-should yes, that guilty yes, that coerced yes, that I-actually-hate-this thing-yes, that I-guess-so yes, that who-else-will-do-it yes, that careless yes, that default

yes, that resentful yes, that I probably-shouldn't but-struggle-with-boundaries yes?

NO. Nope.

This is *exactly* what I needed to hear. Putting it into practice has been nerve-racking but incredibly liberating. I'm a people-pleaser. I want everyone to like me. I want to say yes. I want to meet that need. I want to be the person everyone can count on. While I'm not tossing all those personality traits out completely, I am trying to be more discerning. When someone asks me to do something, I'm pausing, I'm asking the Holy Spirit, should I do this, Lord? Can I handle this? Can I meet this need while still loving and serving my family well? Can I do this without feeling resentful toward the person who asked?

And whoa, he has been so faithful with this new litmus test! After adopting this guiding principle, the owner of the barre studio where I teach asked me to consider teaching some additional classes. I normally teach twice a month on Sunday afternoons, which ends up dominating our Sundays. The class time cuts into our family time even though I do love teaching. The owner asked me to take on an additional weekly morning class and I told her I'd let her know by the end of the day. At first I thought, of course I have to say yes, I should probably teach both. There are two other moms on the schedule who had babies after me but teach more regularly, so I definitely need to get with the program.

Instead, I listened. In my spirit, I knew I needed to say I could do one or the other but not both. I felt the Lord encouraging me to try these new boundaries on for size. I hemmed and I hawed and tried to talk myself into being ok with both classes, but I knew I would end up resentful of the obligation and it would be frustrating for Pete as well. So instead of saying yes like I usually do, I sat down and wrote something to the effect of this:

"It pains me to say this, but this year I'm trying to be more honest with myself and others about what I can and can't do. I want you to know I'm committed and I love being part of the team, so please don't think I'm being flaky, however I can't do both. I'm happy to do whichever one is most helpful to you."

I was so nervous about her reply. The owner is a woman who has a lot on her plate (pregnant, small child, running a business, you know, the usual), and I felt like a jerk for saying I couldn't do more. You know what she said back? She said, and I quote, "Thank you SO much for being honest with me (and yourself!). The Tuesday morning class would be great!" Shezam! It was OK to say no! In fact, it was better than OK. Now I feel happy and excited about when I am going to teach. I don't feel resentful about saying yes to something I didn't really want to do (and I don't have to worry about dragging Pete into the schedule mess I made).

Guiding Principle #3: Make Choices That Give Others Freedom

This brings me to my last point: the lie of COMPARING CAPACITIES. I'll be really honest with you, I spend a lot of my time being overwhelmed. Since becoming a mother, I am easily stressed out, I'm tired, and I just don't have the get-up-and-go I used to have (or that I forced myself to pretend to have). I'm tempted to feel pretty bad about it. I'm frustrated with my capacity. Why do I struggle with being overwhelmed so often when other people seem to thrive while having so much more on their plate? I've got a friend who's running a business, dealing with family health problems, teaching tons of exercise classes, and overseeing a remodel. That's a lot! She's doing it gracefully, of course!

Another friend is an amazing mom, and she's killing it at her job while planning a pinterest-worthy child's birthday party replete with sprinkles, bubbles, balloons, and champagne. Another friend's job is to keep us safe while we lie in bed at night, which she manages with brilliant expertise, and she's also a fantastic wife, neighbor, and a deep spiritual thinker. Geez! How do they all manage this?! Get it together, Natalie!

This is where the enemy wins. If I let these accusing thoughts run rampant, I start to feel like a real loser. You know who's no good to anybody? Women walking around feeling like losers. If we're walking around feeling like losers in the beautiful lives God has given us, we're totally missing out on the special, particular work he has given each of us to do. The enemy wants to steal our joy and make us forget the wonder of *our own* lives. He wants us to believe the lie that we should be looking around us to dictate our days instead of listening to the still, small voice of our Heavenly Father. Right now, my Heavenly Father is telling me to keep it simple.

My aforementioned friend Mae has been a huge help on this journey toward simplicity. She has made some pretty big choices to keep her life simple, and every time she shares them with me, I think, "Oh hey, I could do that too!" Her choices to live simply and not overextend herself (and thus her family) give me the freedom to try it too. She says, "Natalie, when your baby decides to hate the car seat, just don't go anywhere in the car." And I think, "Oh yeah, I guess I could just do that." She and her husband don't make evening commitments during the week. They have two little ones and it just doesn't work for their family right now. They also prioritize rest and time together as a family on the weekends.

What I'm trying to do is make peace with my capacity. Would I rather be stressed and running around trying to juggle a million things because I think I should? Or would I rather take the path God has called me to, and enjoy my life more? Sometimes, we don't get a choice in the burdens or craziness we're asked to bear. Sometimes we do, and I'm choosing simple. Whole days spent in jammies just because I can. Warm baths in the middle of the day just because they're delightful and because bath time with my baby is the most precious, beautiful experience in the whole world. Last but not least, occasionally getting in bed at 7:00 p.m.! Whatever capacity God has given you, make peace with it. Honor your limits. Serve and love others well, but not at the expense of your soul or the well-being of the people you love.

These are my guiding principles for this year. I hope that at the end of the year, I can look back and see God's hand at work through my attempts to simplify, filter, and listen.

Walking with Jesus

On a final note, I want to share an interesting picture the Lord gave me as I was praying. This January, Pete and I committed to embarking on a fast, meaning we are abstaining from alcohol and certain food. We decided to fast because we're asking the Lord about some pretty big changes—location, career, etc. As part of this process, we committed to trying to spend more time praying together. Last night, when we got in bed, we spent about 20 minutes listening to worship music and praying individually, wrote in our journals for a bit, and then shared our thoughts. (Note: This is an unusual occurrence in our home. It was both lovely and surprising. Usually, we don't even talk once we get into bed because we are both wearing earplugs and are ready to fall asleep.)

During this time of listening and praying, the phrase that kept running through my head was, "Whatever you have, Lord." It's a hard thing, to lay all your options down before the throne of grace and say, "Whatever you have, Lord." It's even more difficult to mean it. As soon as I start thinking or praying about one option, my mind takes off at a million miles an hour, calculating timelines and contingency plans and entertaining what ifs. Because he knows what kind of girl I am, the Lord gave me this picture as I was praying last night:

I was a peddler on the street, somewhere on Capitol Hill. I had all the options of where we could go, where we might live, what we might do, placed like little trinkets on a white sheet on the sidewalk before me. I was sitting behind the sheet as someone selling trinkets on the street would sit, but I was fidgeting anxiously. I kept jumping up to rearrange the options, to tweak the positioning of all the things I had laid down, never quite satisfied to leave them alone, untended, on the sheet.

Then Jesus came up to me. He stopped in front of my sheet and looked at me sitting on the ground. He stepped right over the sheet with all my options on it, and extended his hand to me. Helping me up, he said, "Would you like to walk with me?" Surprised yet grateful, I said yes. So we walked off together, leaving the sheet with all my options behind.

Isn't life with God just like that? We think we can manage and arrange and present options to our Heavenly Father, but really, his hope for us is so much bigger than our small minds can even imagine. He invites us to walk with him, to take his hand and set out on the journey together. That's where I want to be. I want to be holding hands with Jesus, wherever that leads me. I don't want to be sitting on the sidewalk fiddling with my options.

God longs to give you boundary lines in pleasant places. His heart is for you to thrive. Ask him where the lines should be; he's waiting to hear from you.

From Cradle to Grave

So I said: 'Do not take me away, O my God, in the midst of my days; your years go on through all generations. In the beginning you laid the foundations of the earth, and the heavens are the work of your hands. They will perish, but you remain; they will all wear out like a garment. Like clothing you will change them and they will be discarded. But you remain the same, and your years will never end. The children of your servants will live in your presence; their descendants will be established before you. (Psalm 102:24–28)

I've been in front of the computer a lot in the last 24 hours. It's far preferable to the *giant* pile of laundry on my guest bed. Plus, I'm waiting on the packets of venison in my sink to defrost to make our first batch of stew from the deer Pete brought home last weekend.

While avoiding my laundry, I've been thinking about the physical cycle of life, about the story God tells through the generations. Sometimes, I'm overcome by grief, mourning the fact that at most only four generations get to be together at one point in time on this side of eternity.

Every few days, our dear friend and neighbor Doc grabs his shaver and heads over to Ms. Ruby's house to give Pops a shave.

Doc has lived in our neighborhood for thirty-six years and we affectionately call him the "Mayor" of Rosedale. He knows all and sees all. He is one of the most generous, helpful, and kindhearted people I have ever met. He co-founded our little Adopt-a-block group with my husband and has become a dear friend. In fact, he was Penny's first babysitter. He usually stops by our house on his way over to Ms. Ruby's, so I've been hearing about Pops, Ms. Ruby, and Miss Stanton for years. They live approximately 100 feet from me but I didn't meet them until a few weeks ago and I'm pretty sure I've been missing out.

Last week, I wept after I got off the phone with my grandmother. She just had her 86th birthday in October and she is the only grandparent Pete and I have left. She's wonderfully spry, whip smart, deep, thoughtful, godly, funny, a little crazy, and above all, one of my very best friends. I count myself immeasurably blessed to consider both my mom and grandmother among my dearest friends. Blood besties are awesome.

My grandmother has experienced much physical pain and illness in her life, not too many horribly serious things, but she has a weak immune system and catches everything. She was joking the other day that she can catch the flu through the telephone. She has handled our family history of depression with grace and aplomb, always bouncing back, fiercely clinging to the Lord. The last two verses of Psalm 27 sum up her tenacity, "I remain confident of this: I will see the goodness of the Lord in the land of the living. Wait for the Lord; be strong and take heart and wait for the Lord."

In the midst of pain she is so joyful! She will tell me about a difficult situation, and I'm thinking, "Yikes! If I were dealing with that, I'd be bowled over," but instead, she will tell me how grateful she is that this and not that happened, or how the Lord is meeting her in the middle of it, or how glad she is to be mobile and alert at 86.

She embodies the thankful life. She's marvelous (one of her favorite words). I could go on for ages.

As we were speaking on the phone recently, she told me how she'd rescued a dozen glorious geraniums from the early Colorado snow, and as she was doing so, she felt a gentle whisper from the Lord to enjoy them, because she might not be here much longer. She's very frank about being ready to go to heaven, but even as she delights in the thought of eternity, she is wonderfully full of joy in her earthly body, which is wearing out. I'm not ready for her to go. I don't want anyone I love to leave me, especially her.

A few hours after speaking with her, I found myself at Ms. Ruby's house with Penny and Sam in tow. Ms. Ruby is Ms. Stanton and Pop's daughter. Ms. Stanton is 100 and Pops is 98. Ms. Stanton still jokes that she nabbed herself a younger man. They've spent almost a century on this earth and seventy-five years by one another's side.

They've raised four children and buried one. Ms. Ruby has converted the whole main level of her home into a bedroom and living area for Ms. Stanton and Pops. The layout of Ms. Ruby's home is the exact same as ours. They have a big bed and a large TV in the area that would be our kitchen. They sit there, day after day together, growing older, weaker, and more immobile. Watching them was beautiful and sad, and I felt confronted with the heavy rush of time.

There I was, wearing my new baby, delicate and fresh, just entering the world, yet one day my body will wear out, her body will wear out, and we will all be called home to Jesus.

I had the privilege of meeting Ms. Ruby as we were leaving. Ms. Ruby is old too! She's probably 75 or 80 herself, and she diligently, lovingly, and sacrificially cares for her parents in her home. That's the way God created the cycle of life. Our parents serve us as we arrive helpless, frail, and small. They nurse us until we get delightful chunky baby thighs. Then we grow older, we become self-sufficient, and as we enter the strength of our youth, the generations above us head toward heaven. "All go to the same place; all come from dust, and to dust all return" (Ecclesiastes 3:20). We begin and end our lives helpless, requiring the loving hands of another to sustain us, to wash us gently, to meet our needs.

I've read the story of Jesus washing the disciples' feet to Penny. It's Jesus' final, tender evening with his disciples. John 13:1, 3–7 says:

> It was just before the Passover Feast. Jesus knew that the time had come for him to leave this world and go to the Father. Having loved his own who were in the world, he now showed them the full extent of his love. Jesus knew that the Father had put all things under his power, and that he had come from God and was returning to God; so he got up from the meal, took off his outer clothing, and wrapped a towel around his waist.

In the *Jesus Storybook Bible*, this story is charmingly adapted for children, yet its simple rendering is no less powerful:

> Jesus and his friends were having the Passover meal together in an upstairs room. But Jesus' friends were arguing. What about? They were arguing about stinky feet. Stinky feet? Yes, that's right. Stinky feet. (Now the thing about feet back then was that people didn't wear shoes; they only wore sandals, which might not sound unusual, except that the streets in those days were dirty—and I don't mean just dusty dirty—I mean really stinky dirty. With all those cows and horses everywhere, you can imagine the stuff on the street that ended up on their feet!)

So, anyway, someone had to wash away the dirt, but it was a dreadful job. Who on earth would ever dream of volunteering to do it?

Only the lowliest servant.

"I'm not the servant!" Peter said.

"Nor am I!" said Matthew.

Quietly, Jesus got up from the table, took of his robe, picked up a basin of water, knelt down, and started to wash his friends' feet.

"You can't," Peter said. He didn't understand about Jesus being the Servant King.

"If you don't let me wash away the dirt, Peter," Jesus said, "you can't be close to me."

Jesus knew that what people needed most was to be clean on the inside. All the dirt on their feet was nothing compared to the sin inside their hearts.

"Then wash me, Lord!" Peter said, tears filling his eyes. "All of me!"

One by one, Jesus washed everyone's feet.

"I am doing this because I love you," Jesus explained.

"Do this for each other."[5]

---

[5]   Lloyd-Jones, Sally. *The Jesus Storybook Bible*. Grand Rapids: Zondervan, 2007.

As you serve the generations above or below you, my prayer is that you would be filled with love and immeasurable grace from our Heavenly Father. As you pour out your love to one another, may he give an unending store of patience and the power to live out his example, enabling you to "do this for each other."

Fearfully and Wonderfully Made

I praise you because I am fearfully and wonderfully made; your works are wonderful, I know that full well. (Psalm 139:14)

Dichotomy: a division or contrast between two things that are or are represented as being opposed or entirely different. [6]

When you have a baby, all of a sudden you have this strange ability to experience the whole kaleidoscope of human emotion at the same time. I am happy and sad, exhausted yet exhilarated, amazed, horrified, and everything in between. This riotous chaos is new and different and a bit perplexing. You have to learn to be comfortable with a contradictory mix of emotions spinning about in your head all the time.

I encountered this contradiction most intensely in relation to my body. Awe and dismay. Reverence and apprehension. I felt a deep respect for my body's ability to grow another human, almost unbidden, in the dark interior of my womb. As biology took over, setting itself to the awesome task of growing a whole separate person, my mind, and its consummate desire for control, had to

---

[6] "Dichotomy." *Dictionary.com*. *www.dictionary.com/browse/dichotomy* (Accessed March 25, 2015).

take a back seat. While experiencing profound wonder, I also found myself loathing the weight gain, hating how my body's changing shape and size suddenly seemed like an appropriate conversation topic to *every single person I encountered*, stranger or friend. For example, every person we met on a cruise: "Oh, are you 8 months pregnant?! No, just five? Huh. Wow."

It's a little weird. And if your relationship with your body has been a bit fraught, it's disconcerting. It brings up old feelings, old insecurities, things you thought you kicked to the curb in the past.

I was a little more comfortable with my body changing during pregnancy because, duh, there's a baby in there. What I was not prepared for was the postpartum experience. Sheesh. The things no one tells you. And it's a kindness, really. But still, completely overwhelming. You look six months pregnant after giving birth for what feels like a super long time. Parts of your body feel like they have undergone irreparable trauma and you wonder how, oh how, you will ever have more children. There are stretch marks in strange places (I'm looking at you, upper inner thighs). You're tired, everything aches all the time, and you just want to devour an entire pan of macaroni and cheese because it's delicious and because the heart wants what the heart wants. You also lack the self control and energy to exercise (unless you are one of those rare creatures who start going to spin classes at four weeks postpartum) because all of your self control is going toward waking up in the middle of the night to feed and care for the tiny, lovely, needy little person who has become the center of your world.

You don't have any leftover time, energy, or will to work out or try to be disciplined. While pregnant, my muffin top turned into a bundt cake and stayed that way for quite a while. Contrary to my anticipatory expectations, I didn't have any get-up-and-go for a long time. I really thought I'd hop back onto the working out wagon, get back in shape super fast, and start feeling back in action. Nope.

However, I did have plenty of time and mental energy to critique my body. A disheartened glimpse in the mirror revealed bags under my eyes that made me look like I got punched in the face, and scores of wrinkles I swear weren't there before I had a baby.

Today, Penny is 7 months old. It's taken a lot longer than I expected to feel like myself again, but I'm slowly emerging from the fog.

Recently, I was talking to one of my girlfriends about having a daughter, and we both expressed our frustration in dealing with body image, wishing we were different or better or done with these stupid issues in our heads and disappointed that we're not quite there yet. I don't want Penny to waste any of the time, energy, or head space that I've wasted over the years wishing she looked different. I don't want her to spend one single second looking in the mirror and not loving what she sees. I want it finished with me. I want so much more for her than I can even believe in for myself. Sometimes, ever so softly, the Holy Spirit whispers to me, "Natalie, that freedom you're praying over her? That blessing? That love? That truth? That's yours too, darling. You can have it too."

So when the hateful body thoughts attack me, I've started whipping out the big guns: lie replacement therapy.

Replacing the lies of the enemy with the truth of God works with any scripture. It breaks open any insidious thought pattern from "I'm not good enough," to "I wish I was like her," to "Ugh, why don't these pants fit yet." The verse I've chosen lately is from Psalm 139:14, "I praise you because I am fearfully and wonderfully made; your works are wonderful, I know that full well."

We are God's workmanship. He knit us together in our mothers' wombs. His work is wonderful. No matter what state we're in, when he looks at us, he says, "Beautiful … this one is good." Mirrors are a baby's (or mom's) best friend—babies love them. When Penny looks at herself in the mirror, she bursts into the most ecstatically joyful smile; she stares and giggles with wonder and abandon. She knows that she is fearfully and wonderfully made. She delights in the image God has given her.

I want to be like that. I want to delight in the way God made me. I want to look in the mirror with joy and wonder.

I'm asking the Lord to help me know "full well" that I am fearfully and wonderfully made, and that as his workmanship, I am beautiful. When I find my mind going to that ugly place, I say Psalm 139:14 over and over to myself, "I praise you because I am fearfully and wonderfully made, I know that full well."

I'm not there yet, but I'm trying.

"So shall my word be that goeth forth out of my mouth: it shall not return unto me void, but it shall accomplish that which I please, and it shall prosper *in the thing* whereto I sent it" (Isaiah 55:11 KJV).

His word does not come back void. He has the power to change the patterns of our mind if we let him. Practice speaking the truth of Scripture over yourself. You are fearfully and wonderfully made, may you know that *full well.*

Equipped for Every Good Work

Whoever dwells in the shelter of the Most High will rest in the shadow of the Almighty. (Psalm 91:1)

Now may the God of peace [the source of serenity and spiritual well-being] who brought up from the dead our Lord Jesus, the great Shepherd of the sheep, through the blood that sealed and ratified the eternal covenant, equip you with every good thing to carry out his will and strengthen you [making you complete and perfect as you ought to be], accomplishing in us that which is pleasing in his sight, through Jesus Christ, to whom be the glory forever and ever. (Hebrews 13:20–21 AMP)

He will gently and carefully lead those nursing their young. (Isaiah 40:11 AMP)

This morning I lingered in a precious moment, cradling the weight of a sleeping baby on my chest. A sweet little life, serene, and completely at peace. Not wriggling or nursing or trying to get down. She was heavy, resting securely in my arms, her soft, downy head snuggled perfectly under my chin.

For a silly, fleeting moment, I thought, "I better put her down, I have that dish in the oven, I need to do that Pilates video, I'm dying for a cup of coffee, and I really want to spend some time with the Lord and perhaps write a little before she wakes up again." And then I realized what utter nonsense was running through my head. Pilates videos, cups of coffee, and to-do lists will forever beckon, but I won't always have my precious daughter resting on my chest.

I savored it, relishing that sweet and ephemeral moment. As I held her, rough and hoarsely whispered prayers tumbled out of my mouth and tears welled up in my eyes. I asked the Lord to bless her and keep her, to cause her to walk in his ways all the days of her life. I begged that she would know, *really know,* how much she is loved by him, *every single day of her life.* I prayed she would walk in her true identity as beloved, because I'm convinced that anyone walking around knowing and feeling how truly loved they are by God is an indomitable force to be reckoned with. I spoke the same prayer over her that my mother has prayed over me every day of my life: that she would be invisible to those who wish her harm, and absolutely, totally visible to those who wish her well.

As I praised the Lord for her tiny, beautiful life, for the swift ferocity with which she took root in my womb, my whispered prayers graduated to pleas that he would equip me to be her mother. I think every mother believes her child is special, because each one is special. Each child is entirely unique, a never-before-seen masterpiece created by God and specially, although painfully, delivered to the family of his choosing, biological or adopted. When I'm asked what my daughter is like, I feel that same swell of pride and that utter conviction that he really knocked it out of the park on this one. Penny is dynamite. My little girl is spark and life and vigor and strength. She's energetic, active, funny, and joyful. She's one of a kind.

I feel the singularity of the opportunity to be her mother deep in my bones. She's the only one of her and I'm her only mother. I'm awestruck and overwhelmed with the weight of this calling, this privilege. I desperately want to love her well. I found myself uttering, "Help me do right by her," a phrase that has never before occurred to me, and one I felt a bit ridiculous saying, but I meant it. I want to do right by her, but I don't even know how to begin. However, God, her true father, her creator, her savior, her friend, he knows exactly what she needs. He will help me love her well. The Holy Spirit, our helper, lives within us, enabling us to walk in the power we have through Christ Jesus.

We are not standing alone, staring up at the gargantuan mountains we are asked to climb. The Holy Spirit, our prescient, ever-prepared guide has all the stuff we need for the journey. His pack is full of ropes and chisels, climbing boots, headlamps, and astronaut foodstuffs. He knows how to Belay On (Did I have to look up climbing commands on REI.com? Yes, I did. You're welcome).[7] He has all the equipment you need for the climb held securely in his hand.

My dear women, whatever mountain you're facing, whether a short-term climb or a lifelong endeavor, know that you are fully equipped for what is required of you. You need only ask your Heavenly Father for the strength he has made readily available to you in the Holy Spirit.

---

[7]   Wood, T.D. "Communication for Climbing." Last updated March 25, 2015. *Learn at REI*. <u>www.rei.com</u>. (Accessed March 25, 2015).

He Did Not Entrust Himself To Them

> Now while he was in Jerusalem at the Passover Feast, many people saw the miraculous signs he was doing and believed in his name. But Jesus would not entrust himself to them, for he knew all men. He did not need man's testimony about man, for he knew what was in a man. (John 2:23–24)

Being a mom is by far the most difficult thing I have ever undertaken. The sheer unpredictability of another little human, the sleep deprivation, and again, the unpredictability—all of it has thrown me for a loop. Even several months in, the same day-in, day-out activities—feed baby, try to get baby to sleep, play with baby—can still feel so overwhelming to me, especially when said baby is screaming at me. I continually get frustrated at myself for being surprised at how difficult things feel. Sometimes we have great weeks, but other times, like this past week, it's very challenging.

Even after many months of this roller coaster, I'm surprised by these challenging weeks, and then mad at myself for being surprised. Like, "Come on, Natalie, when are you just going to get it that there is no guarantee that once you have a good week, you will continue to have only good weeks? You have to accept the good weeks when they happen (or moments, or hours, or one-off nights of good sleep) and the rest of the time know that the only constant is change." The Lord and I will probably be working on this concept of the constancy of change for the rest of my life. Today, he reminded me of a particular piece of this puzzle.

Becoming a parent presents myriad opportunities to compare yourself to others. Satan offers countless invitations to feel bad about yourself, your choices, your abilities, your contribution to society or the Kingdom or whatever else there is to feel bad about. The last week or so, I have been accepting these invitations to sprint down the unhealthy rabbit trails in my mind. These invitations to feel bad about myself are based on earthly standards, on perceptions about what I or my baby "should" be doing or not doing, and not based on my worth and identity in Christ. Only Jesus has the power to say who I am and over and over again he says, "You are my beloved." This morning, the Lord offered me another invitation, and I desperately wanted to accept it.

As you know, I am reading through the Bible on a multi-year nonplan, and this morning I was in Psalm 56 and John 2. In John 2, Jesus is just beginning his ministry in the temple. He is in Jerusalem at the Passover Feast where he's starting to get some traction. People are into it and it's the perfect time to start feeling good about himself. Yet he doesn't take the bait to feel good about himself based on other people's approval. Their approbation doesn't matter to him. He knows the deeply fickle heart of man.

> Now while he was in Jerusalem at the Passover
> Feast, many people saw the miraculous signs he was
> doing and believed in his name. But Jesus would
> not entrust himself to them, for he knew all men.
> He did not need man's testimony about man, for he
> knew what was in a man (John 2:23–24).

Jesus did not *entrust himself to them*. He refused to take the bait and rest his worth and self-esteem on how the world viewed him. I want to be able to say to the voices of other people or the voices in my head, "I do not accept what you say about me. Good or bad, praise or persecution, only God's voice matters." I don't want to entrust myself to the world; I want to entrust myself to God.

In Psalm 56, David reminds us that only God is trustworthy, and that only his voice and his Word matter:

> When I am afraid, I will trust in you. In God, whose word I praise, in God I trust; I will not be afraid. What can mortal man do to me? In God, whose word I praise, in the Lord, whose word I praise—in God I trust I will not be afraid. What can man do to me? I am under vows to you, O God; I will present my thank offerings to you. For you have delivered me from death and my feet from stumbling that I may walk before God in the light of life (Psalm 56:3–4, 10–13).

At first glance, it seems like David might just be worried about men who are out to get him. Indeed, he probably was worried about flesh and blood foes but there's another layer of application. When David says, "what can mortal man do to me," it's not just about what man can do by harming us physically, but what man can do to us with ungodly expectations, with invitations to feel insufficient, or with comparison threatening to rob us of our joy.

We don't have to be afraid or succumb to these voices or expectations. We don't have to accept the invitations to feel bad. We don't have to entrust ourselves to men and their thoughts and opinions. Instead, we can trust that the Lord will give us the strength to believe what he says about us. He says some good stuff. He says we are redeemed, worthy, and that we are called and created uniquely according to his purposes. You can rest and be still in exactly the season he has you in, however insignificant it may seem or however frustrated you might feel at your attempts to accomplish everyday life. Entrust yourself to God. His thoughts toward you are what matter. His words to you bring life.

Here's what he's saying. I'll repeat it over and over and over again, until I'm blue in the face. He's saying, "I love you. Come to me. You are worthy through my sacrifice. I have redeemed you. I have called you by name. You are mine" (portions from Isaiah 43:1).

If you've never read the children's book, *Wherever You Are My Love Will Find You* by Nancy Tillman, buy it, read it, memorize it. The book was a baby shower gift from my friend and I still cry every time I read it to Penny. It's beautifully written and exquisitely illustrated. The story is told in the title: wherever you are, my love will find you. It's written from the perspective of a loving parent, but the story reads like a love letter from God. In particular, this portion has stayed with me, "In the green of the grass ... in the smell of the sea ... in the clouds floating by ... at the top of a tree ... in the sound crickets make at the end of the day ... 'You are loved. You are loved. You are loved,' they all say."

You are loved. You are loved. You are loved.

The Way from No to Yes

For I was hungry, and you fed me. I was thirsty, and you gave me a drink. I was a stranger, and you invited me into your home. (Matthew 25:35)

Do not forget to show hospitality to strangers, for by so doing some people have shown hospitality to angels without knowing it. (Hebrews 13:12)

What is more, I consider everything a loss because of the surpassing worth of knowing Christ Jesus my Lord, for whose sake I have lost all things. I consider them garbage, that I may gain Christ. (Philippians 3:8)

On Saturday morning at 5:00 a.m., I found myself chatting with two complete strangers in my living room while I puttered in the kitchen making coffee, splendidly attired in my lipstick jammies and polka-dotted blue fleece robe. How, you may ask, did I get myself in this particular predicament? I'm pretty adept at getting myself into awkward, over-extended social pickles, and this morning was no exception. Later, I texted a few girlfriends that I had two strange women sleeping in my basement and they were not at all surprised. This scenario was not even close to the most outlandish situation I've gotten myself into, which is saying something.

Let's back up 7 weeks to when my perky daughter started waking up at 5:00 a.m. At first, we were horrified, it was like being ripped out of our deepest REM and thrust into starting the day in the middle of the night. It was unconscionable and I was super mad about it. I read all the sleep blogs, we tried earlier bedtimes, later bedtimes, different foods, supplementing before bed, shifted nap schedules, you name it, all to no avail. My early-bird daughter would sleep through the night (bless her) and wake up raring to go at 5:00 a.m. I had been trying for months to become a morning person, and I thought that maybe this was some twisted way the Lord was helping me become a morning person very much against my will.

By the time my path crossed with these two lovely women, we had just made peace with the fact that Penny gets up at 5:00 a.m. In fact, in the rare instance she ever slept later, we would still wake up early. This explains why, at 4:30 in the morning when we heard loud banging next door, I was already lying in bed awake. Finally, the persistent knocking on the front door roused my husband, who, in exact opposition to what I would have done, politely stuck his head out the window and said, "Can I help you ladies with something?" in a kind and almost apologetic tone.

If anyone, and I do mean *anyone,* wakes me up in the middle of the night with loud music or other inappropriate nighttime pursuits, I am for sure going to yell at them. This includes the scary drug dealers who used to live next door. I marched over there at 3:00 a.m., banged on the door and told them to keep it down without a second thought. Another episode involves an incessantly beeping disconnected fire alarm but it contains more expletives than I care to record for posterity. Don't mess with my sleep. Don't even think about it. So these ladies were lucky that (a) I was already awake and thus not mad about it and (b) Pete's side of the bed is closer to the window.

Back to 4:30 a.m. The ladies said they were locked out of their

Airbnb and politely apologized for waking him. Pete got back in bed and said, "I feel like we should let them in, it's really cold outside and they're stuck out there." To which I responded, "You can't invite them in, they'll think you're some stranger creeper, I'll go downstairs since I'm already dead awake!" So I went downstairs and persuaded them to come inside. It took some cajoling, but since they had been outside for a while without coats in thirty-degree weather, I eventually won them over—I'm guessing this was in large part due to my non-threatening lipstick-patterned PJs. Turns out their friends had fallen asleep and accidentally locked them out. They were in a strange town, locked out of a strange house in more or less the middle of the night, and they were cold and tired.

They came inside and got settled while I made breakfast. I had baked oatmeal on hand and I made some scrambled eggs for us. As we sat down to eat, one of the women asked me, "Do you believe in God? Because right now, I'm observing Lent, and you inviting us in is making me believe that God is real." We proceeded to have a wonderful and honest conversation about faith and I shared a little bit about what the Lord had done in my life recently. We rejoiced in his goodness and marveled at how he meets our needs. I said, "Isn't it cool that God knew you were going to need a place to get warm and he also knew that I have a penchant for inviting strangers into my home?" He sees us, down to the last detail. It feels pretty wonderful to be seen, really seen, down to the minutest detail, by the God of the universe.

A little bit later, I packed them off to our basement guest room because they needed some sleep. Lucky for them, I had put the entire bed back together with freshly washed sheets, pillowcases, and the duvet cover earlier in the week while I was avoiding Penny's nap strike upstairs. They slept for a few hours until their friends finally woke up and came looking for them. The early morning ladies graciously said goodbye and left to enjoy the rest of their weekend in DC. They were kind enough to send us an Edible Arrangement as a thank-you gift, which was hilarious, because Pete and I saw the Edible Arrangements truck on our way home from church and we both said, "Those things are so strange, how do they even stay in business? Who buys them?" When we got home our neighbor said, "Hey! This was getting delivered to you and I said I'd keep it in the fridge until you got home." It was a giant Edible Arrangement.

Their brief stay with us got me thinking about a few things. First, what does it look like to practice hospitality? Was this an instance where I appropriately practiced hospitality or did I exceed my own or others' boundaries in my compulsive propensity to overextend? Thankfully, my honest answer was that it was the perfect opportunity to extend hospitality. I didn't feel drained or burdened by it, and I think they felt grateful and blessed. I'm not writing this to say that we're awesome or that you should go looking for more strangers to sleep in your basement. I struggle with boundaries, mostly with myself, and it's an area of my life that I unquestionably need to turn over to the Lord. So in this instance, I'm happy to report that I think we did the right thing.

The other thing that came to mind was the unlikely sequence of events. If Penny hadn't been waking up regularly at such an ungodly hour, there's no way I would have been awake. If those perfectly nice ladies had roused me from my sweet Saturday slumber, I would *not* have said anything polite out of the window, and would have altogether missed the opportunity to invite them into our home. Maybe Penny waking up early for weeks on end had all been for that moment at the breakfast table where one of the women said definitively, "You inviting us in makes me know that God is real." Maybe morning after exhausting morning was all leading up to that, maybe it wasn't. If the sole purpose behind my sleep deprivation was that one moment in time where I was able to be the hands and feet of

Jesus for two women, was it worth it? Would I sign up for it? Would I do it with a willing heart? Would I even do it again?

Let's be clear. Waking up at 5:00 a.m. is not suffering. Plenty of people do it all the time. The answer to not being sleep deprived is pretty simple, go to bed earlier. But it still felt like a sacrifice to me. I wondered what my response would have been if the Lord had given this assignment ahead of time, saying, "Natalie, your child will wake up at 5:00 a.m. for many months because in 7 weeks' time, you will encounter two women who need to know that God is real at 4:30 in the morning. And you will invite them into your home." I probably would have said, "Seriously, Lord? Isn't there a better way to do this? Surely, I don't need to wake up this early for months to meet this need, right?"

Then I checked myself and realized, "Wait, aren't we supposed to give up *everything* for the gospel? And give it up joyfully, as well?" My attitude is not nearly as aligned with what the gospel requires of us as I'd like to think.

Philippians 3:8 says, "What is more, I consider everything a loss because of the surpassing worth of knowing Christ Jesus my Lord, for whose sake I have lost all things. I consider them garbage, that I may gain Christ." Do I consider everything a loss (including my sleep) because of the surpassing worth of knowing Christ Jesus my Lord? Would I do anything he asked of me in the hopes that one of his beloved children might see that he is real through some small action of mine? My answer is probably no, but I want my answer to be yes. I want my answer to be, "Yes, Lord! Whatever you ask of me, I will do it joyfully!" I'll confess I struggle with the way from no to yes. But I know the One who knows the way and we're working on it.

Honor One Another Above Yourselves

Honor one another above yourselves ... Practice hospitality. (Romans 12:10, 13)

Today I finally met up with a girlfriend to enjoy the pedicure she gave me as a birthday gift. It's March. My birthday is in October, but that's life these days, and it was kind of nice to prolong the celebration. Pedicure on a rainy Saturday? Check! Girlfriends chatting in the old-school hair salon fashion with everyone getting their nails done chiming in? Check! Requisite trip to TJ Maxx for the completely miscellaneous yet somehow totally necessary bag of stuff? Check! Check! (I'm talking about you, baby fridge magnets, I totally needed you in my life. Seriously baby fridge magnets are so entertaining which = mom actually cooking dinner!)

As we were getting our nails done, the subject of manners came up, specifically, which things are nonnegotiable? Which etiquette niceties make you happy to give and receive? It's a great question to pose to a group, especially since we're in DC and most of us grew up in different parts of the country, each with its own social quirks.

It's so interesting to see what tops the list. For one friend, she always notices if someone says, "Please pass the salt," and the other person just passes the salt, or passes both the salt and the pepper.

I've been through my fair share of etiquette classes, and I'm sure I learned you're supposed to pass both, but if I did, I certainly don't recall. Now that we've all read this, hopefully we'll remember to pass both the salt and the pepper. I have another friend from Minnesota, and in her family, breaking the bread before buttering it was rigorously enforced. I've never heard of that one, but I'm sure it's the proper thing to do.

I have three things that rise to the top of my list. Immediate hospitality, thank-you notes, and RSVPs. To me, immediate hospitality means that when someone walks in my door, I offer them something to drink, hopefully a snack or two, and inquire about their day. I try to supply tea, coffee, water, gin & soda, etc., usually offered in that order, and perhaps a treat from a recent culinary endeavor. It's not much, but it makes me feel at home when I'm offered the same courtesies and I want guests to feel at ease right when they arrive.

I also love me some thank-you notes. Fancy personalized stationery makes me want to whip out my credit card. I like writing notes and I like receiving them. Sitting down to express your heartfelt thanks in writing is a truly irreplaceable exercise, only to be surpassed by the writing of a really great birthday card. My mom has a little ritual she does whenever she's facing a mountain of paperwork and I've adopted it for writing thank-you notes. I light a pretty candle, make a cup of tea, and break out my special pens for correspondence. I received these gorgeous pens as law school graduation presents, presumably to sign important legal documents. Since my days are now mostly occupied with playdates, diapers, and cooking, I use these pens to express my gratitude.

Now let's talk about RSVPs. I am obsessed with RSVPs and positively aggressive about them. Part of the obsession is the irrational anxiety that I will throw a party and no one will come, like that story in the Bible where the King throws a big party and invites everyone but they're all too busy to attend. The other part is trying to figure out how much food to make and how many beverages to have on hand. Lastly, it's just good manners! Somehow, in DC, perhaps because there are so many things to be invited to and many of the invitations are now by e-mail, people don't think they need to RSVP. Wrong, you *must* RSVP. I wish I could say I'm always perfect in all of these etiquette categories, but I'm not, and I've definitely dropped the ball on RSVPs, but I assure you, I was appropriately mortified.

Manners and etiquette play fascinating roles within marriages. In our circle of friends, we have several geographically mixed marriages, which means etiquette is frequently a topic that creates marital discord (of the heated, if friendly, variety). We've got a southern belle married to a cut-off wearing, tactical-pant-loving Midwestern boy (with a man bun!). We've got our palindrome couple, a polite Carolina girl married to an exuberant Southern California bro. And yours truly, a West Coast is the best coast girl married to an English boy who grew up in the Carolinas. I'm sure you can imagine the spirited discussions about etiquette, manners, and best practices in these households.

In fact, our palindrome couple regularly conducts a group text poll on important matters such as, "When you address your child's pediatrician do you say 'Dr.' + their full name? Or just address them as 'Doctor?'" The other couples in this circle all grew up in the same states and mostly agree on etiquette, aside from the seemingly boundless chasm between what men think is appropriate and what women deem necessary when it comes to manners.

Our southern belle and Midwestern manly man have the liveliest debates. Etiquette is such a regular topic of conversation in their household that she asked for and received the most recent edition of *Emily Post's Etiquette*. With its golden gilt and embossed leather cover, it makes a beautiful statement piece, prominently displayed on the coffee table so she can regularly refer to, and he can adamantly dispute, its contents.

One evening early in their marriage, he came downstairs in his painting work jeans and the undershirt he had been wearing to work that day, ready to entertain their small group for dinner. She looked at him in utter bewilderment and asked him if he was going to plumb something. When he said no, he just wanted to be comfortable, she said, "Well, at least go put a shirt on before people start arriving." He said, "But this is a shirt!" And she pulled the collar up to read the label, "See how this says Hanes underwear? It's not a shirt. It's underwear. If you think this is a shirt, next time I'm coming to Bible study in my bra." I'd love to be a fly on the wall in their home.

Back to the nail salon. As we were chatting about manners, we all agreed on one thing. Manners should not be about what's right and what's wrong, or provide us with arcane and occasionally conflicting rules to use as a bludgeon to indict the behavior of others. Etiquette is about making other people feel comfortable, honored, and welcome. Manners are a kind of love language. They are a tangible way to love, appreciate, and honor the people in our homes and our lives.

The second a dinner party begins to be about you, your home, your culinary skills, and your excellence, you've missed the intended purpose of hospitality. It goes the other direction as well. If you're so obsessed with your home not being clean or pretty or perfect enough that you refuse to open the front door, you're missing half the beauty of having a home. Homes are for welcoming, manners are for making other people feel at ease, and etiquette provides the general framework in which we all attempt the funny but necessary social dance of interacting with each other.

In Romans 12:13, Paul calls us to, "practice hospitality," in the broader context of personal responsibility, love, and offering our bodies up as living sacrifices. In verse 10, he exhorts believers to "Honor one another above yourselves," meaning hospitality isn't about us. It's about honoring the guest by anticipating what will make them feel comfortable and special. Honoring others with our hospitality may even mean exercising restraint when you know an over-the-top event will make someone feel small and incapable of reciprocating, rather than cherished and loved.

In verse 9, Paul says, "Love must be sincere." Just as our love must be sincere, our hospitality must be sincere and our manners must be genuine. We need to mean the welcome, we need to be ready in our hearts for the interaction. That doesn't mean you won't feel pulled or stretched or challenged. True hospitality isn't easy, and it doesn't always mean hanging out with people we like who are like us. In fact, true hospitality is often radical and redemptive in the way that only stretching and beautiful things can be. But if the attitude of our hearts isn't up to the task, we'll be more like resounding gongs and clanging symbols than bearers of love. Part of addressing your attitude is figuring out what you can reasonably do in love.

For years, I entertained out of my league, planning big dinner parties or attempting complicated meals because I grew up with a mother who gives Martha Stewart a run for her money. I also have a circle of friends who are exceptionally gifted hostesses. It was so stressful! I'd be yelling at my husband, running around like a crazy lady, furiously speed cleaning, cooking, cursing. Then I'd have to paste a big fake smile on my face when guests arrived. I've learned the hard way, and I do mean the hard way (especially since having a baby), to try to entertain in a way that allows me to practice low-key and welcoming hospitality.

Right now that means more snacks to assemble (thank you Trader Joe's!) and less elaborate cooking. It means more impromptu get-togethers and fewer events planned far in advance. It also means fewer people in our home because (a) it's super tiny, and (b) cooking for large groups stresses me out. Just because I grew up learning exactly what it takes to execute a lavish soiree does not mean that every time I entertain it has to be at that level. My mother is a truly gifted hostess. She's thoughtful about details and surprises in a way I can never emulate. It's her love language. She loves to throw parties and make people feel special and she is *so good* at it.

I enjoy it too, but not in the same way. And I'm gradually learning to ignore that little voice inside my head that says, "This isn't good enough, you can do better, you know how to do better." That little voice wants me to shut the front door and lock the iron gate. It wants me to focus on myself and how others will perceive me rather than how I can live a life of welcoming hospitality. Let's ignore that little voice and keep the door open, shall we?

Stay in the Kitchen

Jesus loved Martha and her sister and Lazarus. Yet when he heard that Lazarus was sick, he stayed where he was two more days. (John 11:5–6)

Lately I've been having a bunch of recipe fails and I am so over it. Cooking is time-consuming, shopping is a hassle with a baby, but eating is a requirement. When I actually make something from real food, turn on my oven, and try to chop onions wearing my onion goggles on my teensy tiny countertops, it needs to work. I don't have time to make mediocre meals, and I certainly don't have time to make flops. Plus, there is nothing worse than making a *giant* pot of lentil soup that looks like sludge but tastes only slightly better, and then realizing that you don't have time to cook again for a few days and you'll be eating that for lunch and dinner until Wednesday. Nobody has time for that.

For instance, I delayed my quiet time this morning so I could whip up some delicious breakfast for Penny and Pete to feast upon when they returned from their weekly Saturday morning date. I had a few gorgeous Meyer lemons. Meyer lemons are my favorite, favorite lemons, and I asked Pete to pretty please plant me a Meyer lemon tree one day if we live somewhere that actually has dirt and sunshine. I had these beautiful lemons and I found a pretty food blog with a recipe for Meyer lemon coconut bread, which sounds delicious, right? Wrong! Sub-par at best! And kind of annoying because we have to keep our baking supplies in a plastic box in the basement so the mice won't get into them (Gross, I know. Thanks, DC.). I had to haul up my flour and sugar and get out one million bowls, bake for 45 minutes, and all this for a dud? Nope. Not cool. Don't have time for that.

This insult to injury is compounded by the fact that I was very ambitious this morning and decided to add a Swiss chard and egg casserole to the mix. Not only did it fail to bake in the allotted time (egg casseroles always take *forever* to bake), it was astoundingly mediocre! Edible, certainly, but not delicious and the goal is food that is delicious. Furthermore, earlier this week I doubled a chocolate pot de creme recipe, which made *eighteen* pot de cremes (way too many for my event!). I sullied *every single bowl I own* for the process. They weren't even that good. They were kind of grainy and the flavor was just ok. Definitely edible, but not delicious. The pot de cremes might have been my fault, because a girlfriend used the exact same recipe with delicious results. I tried the fruit of her labor, and can attest that they were divine. I'll concede the pot de cremes, but my cooking flops can't all be me! I do sometimes make delicious food, so at least some of the recipes have to be duds. That's my story and I'm sticking to it.

Recipe flops and failures aside, since my family needs to eat, I'm staying in the kitchen. Staying in the kitchen is a concept perfectly illustrated in *Live a Praying Life* ®, the aforementioned prayer study by Jennifer Kennedy Dean. This study is thoroughly and utterly transforming the way I think about prayer. You know when you start a book and think, "Whoa, this one goes in the lifetime library. I won't be the same after I read this." This book makes the cut.

In the chapter entitled, "Waiting on God," the author draws out fantastic examples from Scripture and I was particularly struck by her explanation of the story of Mary, Martha, and Lazarus:

John, as he tells the story [of Lazarus], sets the stage with these words: *'Now Jesus loved Martha and her sister and Lazarus'* (John 11:5 NASB). Why do you think he put that sentence in? I think it was because of what comes next. *'Now Jesus loved Martha and her sister and Lazarus. So when He heard that he was sick, He then stayed two days longer in the place where He was'* (John 11:5-6 NASB). John wanted to make it clear that when Jesus built a delay into the process, when He stayed two days longer in the place where He was, it was in the context of how much He loved Martha, Mary, and Lazarus ... If Jesus had come to Bethany and healed Lazarus before he died, Mary's and Martha's prayer would have been answered. Their faith in Jesus would have been affirmed. They would have been more certain than ever that Jesus is Lord over illness. But they would never have known that Jesus is Lord over death. The Father is always teaching us the lordship of Jesus in deeper, more experiential ways ... When it appears from earth that God is delaying, He is really putting pieces together that you had not thought of. He is engineering circumstances so that His power and glory will be on display. When God builds a waiting period into the course of your affairs, it means that what He is doing requires it. **His apparent delays are loving, purposeful, and deliberate.**[8]

I love the way she draws out what Jesus is doing in his apparent

---

[8] Dean, Jennifer Kennedy. *Live a Praying Life.* Anniversary Edition. ©2010 Jennifer Kennedy Dean *Live a Praying Life®* is published by New Hope Publishers. All Rights Reserved.

delay. If Jesus hadn't waited, the disciples and all the mourners who gathered to support Mary and Martha would not have seen that he is Lord over death! Lord over sickness, yes, but not Lord over death. When we start looking at apparent delays through this lens, it totally reorients our thinking.

Instead of focusing on the delay, despairing that God must have forgotten us, or won't answer our prayers because of some vague cosmic reason we will never know, we can start thinking about apparent delays as bigger than us. God is always bringing all things together for the good of those who love him (Romans 8:28), so *he is working on our behalf.* Often, when the passage of time takes more and more options off the table, it becomes less about our own capabilities and more about his power.

If we stop praying, we miss out on the process. We miss the chance to see God's hand at work, to rest in his presence, fully assured of his lordship over timing and our lives. Kennedy Dean likens the discipline of praying while waiting to staying in the kitchen while breakfast is being made. If we opt out of prayer in seasons of waiting, we miss the process, we lack the assurance that he's working on it because we've left the kitchen altogether. Staying in the kitchen won't necessarily speed up the timing of God's process but it allows us to *see* the process.

Prayer is staying in the kitchen. It's knowing that your need has been heard and will be answered at the right time and in the right way. When I'm in the midst of a delay, I'm so tempted to give up. I want to storm out of the kitchen, muttering that the oven must be broken because nothing is cooking in my life. But on my best days, and in my heart of hearts, I want to stay in the kitchen. I want to perch on a stool at the counter, fingers curled around a warm mug of coffee, cozy in my PJs, chatting with God about the day while he makes me breakfast. Both physically and spiritually, I'm staying in the kitchen because a girl's gotta eat!

In the sweetest turn of events, guess what happened a few days later? I had shared my lemon debacle with a few friends, and one dear soul took pity on my culinary endeavors and decided to give me another try. On a cold, snowy night, I quickly reached outside to grab the mail. Much to my surprise, a little white box addressed to Natalie "In the Kitchen" was waiting for me with six gorgeous Meyer lemons inside! They smelled fresh and delicious, like heaven, like California. My dear friend Ellen sent me lemons from her tree. Her generosity meant I got a second chance in the kitchen, a bit like the way we get a second chance because of the generosity of Christ's sacrifice for us. Through him, we receive a gift we never deserved, we get a second chance to live a life that's different, that means something. There's nothing better than a bright, fresh surprise in the middle of winter—a reminder that our God is good and full of grace.

Stay in kitchen, dearest. It's cozy in the kitchen. You're safe in his presence. He's working on your behalf and he wants you to be part of the process. Trust him as you wait. Draw on his power to enable you to persevere.

Rejoice with Those Who Rejoice

Rejoice with those who rejoice; mourn with those
who mourn. (Romans 12:15)

Penny has been up since 4:50 a.m. this morning. Yes, you
read that right, 4:50 a.m.! Pete is in Atlanta briefly for work so I'm
flying solo, but graciously, miraculously, I feel great right now. This
morning, I only felt like a small Car2Go hit me and not a semi-truck.

My heart is happy and here is why:

The last two weeks have been filled with wonderful things
happening for dear friends. A long and difficult season came to
a joyous close, culminating in an are-you-kidding-is-this-for-real
kind of job offer for a nearest and dearest. A precious and selfless
friend enjoyed tender and specific answers to prayer as she gave
birth to another couple's child.

I have prayed for these women and their situations for months
and months. Even though the answers to these prayers aren't actually
happening to me, I'm rejoicing like they are! In a way, they are
happening to me. Since I have lifted them up in prayer, I am invited
to be a partner in seeing God's mighty hand at work. I've been face
down on my knees on their behalf, so their joy is my joy.

We are specifically called to this communal experience of joy.
We are to rejoice with those who rejoice and mourn with those who
mourn. I think it's often easier to mourn with those who mourn.

When something sad happens, we circle the wagons, we hunker down together and we sit in the sadness. We carry the weight and the burden, and we hope that by sharing in it just a little, we have eased the pain of someone we love. Envy, that brutal, ugly beast that lurks in the dark corners of our hearts, does not rear its lying head quite so often when we mourn with one another.

But rejoicing. True rejoicing in the blessings of others requires a particular kind of knowledge, a certainty of the character of God. Rejoicing with others requires a kind of knowledge that speaks of experiential veracity—you need to know that you know that God is good and will provide for you. Without that deep knowledge of his character and his love for you, it's tempting to fall prey to envy.

It's easy to share in one another's joy when that joy doesn't really apply to you, or when it's separate and altogether non-threatening. It's much harder to rejoice when someone gets what you want. The friend who becomes pregnant easily when you've been trying for years. The professional success of a peer who doesn't seem to be working as hard as you are. Or financial success that comes so easily to someone else. Or the physical health you've been asking the Lord for but haven't yet received. These situations make it difficult to rejoice because envy is always at the ready, asking, "Hey! What about me?"

Envy is a thief and a robber. Envy wants to cut you out of the deal. Envy wants to block the invitation to share in one another's joy as God answers prayers and blesses those around us.

In 1 Corinthians 12, Paul talks about the body of Christ—one body with many parts, each with its own specific purpose and calling, not one part more important than the other. Verse 26 says, *"If one part suffers, every part suffers with it; if one part is honored, every part rejoices with it."* We are of one body. We are seeking one mind, the mind of Christ. As one body, we can rejoice with each other as God answers prayer, strengthens our frames, and proves himself faithful. It is such a delight to expand the realm of God's glory in my life. Instead of just focusing on my needs, my wants, my prayer requests, when I lift up my sisters and friends, I get to say, **"Look at what my God did! Do you see that? Look at how beautiful that is!"**

I'm happy to report that for these two women, it's been so easy for me to rejoice. It's been pure, unadulterated joy. But I want to rejoice even when it's difficult for me to rejoice. I want to be pointing all over the place, "See what he did? We asked for that and he did it!"

When we enter into the sorrows and joys of others, when we intercede on their behalf, seeking God's favor for their good, we get invited to the celebration feast. I don't know about you, but I want more of that in my life. I want a share of that joy.

The Comfort Food of Sin

Do not store up for yourselves treasures on earth, where moth and rust destroy, and where thieves break in and steal. But store up for yourselves treasures in heaven, where moth and rust do not destroy, and where thieves do not break in and steal. For where your treasure is, there your heart will be also.

The eye is the lamp of the body. If your eyes are good, your whole body will be full of light. But if your eyes are bad, your whole body will be full of darkness. If then the light within you is darkness, how great is that darkness! No one can serve two masters. Either he will hate the one and love the other, or he will be devoted to the one and despise the other. You cannot serve both God and Money.

Therefore I tell you, do not worry about your life, what you will eat or drink; or about your body, what you will wear. Is not life more important than food, and the body more important than clothes. (Matthew 6:19–25)

My friend Hayley likes to talk about skills in terms of superpowers. She insists everybody has one, and that her particular superpower is recognizing other people's superpowers. It's true, she's dynamite at identifying exactly what people are meant to do, and it's quite a gift. She has other lesser superpowers, and one of them is naming things. If you ever need to name anything—a yacht, a child, an obscure trend, she is your girl. Crafty titles are her specialty. I won the friend lottery with her about fifteen years ago, before either of us realized how cool, edgy, and interesting she would become, and how uncool, fairly traditional, and conformist I would remain.

One cold and rainy night we were on the phone talking about her recent move to New York and how hard it is to start over. She expressed frustration that the same sins, the same insidious ways of thinking keep entrapping her. I jumped in to commiserate, since we share the same default settings. Out of her mouth came this brilliant phrase, "It's like envy is my comfort food of sin. It's the place I keep coming back to. It's like tucking into macaroni and cheese, or curling up in a favorite cashmere sweater. It's where I feel comfortable." Not one to miss out on an opportunity to capitalize on her superpower, I said, "Hey, can I steal your phrase and write about that?" Like the generous person she is, she let me appropriate her brilliance.

Envy is a shape-shifting, hungry beast that is never satisfied. As soon as you obtain whatever it is you've been envying, happiness is snatched out of your reach as something uglier and deeper, and of course, more attractive, sprouts to take its place. Frustratingly, I seem to fall for it every time.

When all our friends started buying houses, I desperately wanted to own a home. The Lord provided and we bought our first house. I was elated and so happy ... until other people started buying bigger and better houses and remodeling and suddenly my house looked kind of crappy by comparison. The cycle *never* ends. There's always the next thing, there's always someone or something better waiting around the corner to make you feel bad about what you've got. I remember thinking so distinctly in my second year of law school, "If we just hit this number for Pete's salary, it will be enough, we will finally not have to worry about money." We hit that number and shocker, it was nice, but not enough for everything, not enough to keep me from fantasizing about the next number, the next thing.

I'm finally old enough to realize that envy leaves me empty, unsatisfied, and incapable of enjoying any of the glorious gifts God has given me. I have a long way to go, but I'm recognizing the lie. The belief that everything would be fine if I could just get my hands on the object of my envy *is a lie from the pit of hell.* You heard me, *a lie from the pit of hell.* It is a powerful and destructive fallacy. Believing this lie threatens to rob you of recognizing the goodness of God in every corner of your life. Envy will constantly keep you running on the hamster wheel of comparison, whatever that may look like to you. Proverbs 14:30 puts it best, "A heart at peace gives life to the body, but envy rots the bones." Freshman year of college, my roommate wrote this quote from Theodore Roosevelt in lipstick on our full-length mirror, "Comparison is the thief of joy." The relevance and truth of this statement resonated in my mind immediately, but the journey from the mind to the heart is a more complicated endeavor.

Before we delve deeper into envy, let's indulge a brief sidebar on the purpose and intent of healing prayer, and perhaps silence that alarm going off in your head, "Whoa! Healing prayer! What kind of weirdo is she?! Close the book, I'm done."

Our church has a strong healing prayer ministry, and I have benefited enormously from both the teaching on healing prayer and healing prayer appointments with members of the prayer team. Healing prayer appointments in our church aren't anything mystical or magical. They are tools in the spiritual tool belt. Healing prayer provides an opportunity to meet with two devoted, trained, and equipped people who help you pray through whatever issues or challenges you may be facing. Using God's Word and his promises, they invite the Holy Spirit in to deal with the topic of the appointment, asking the Holy Spirit to replace areas of struggle or sin with the truth of God.

The analogy that helps me the most is to think of yourself as an old house. When we become Christians, Christ literally purchases us with his blood. We are his, irrevocably and for all eternity (justification). Even though Christ owns the house, there may be termites in the attic, spiders in the basement, and a leaky pipe under the kitchen sink. The house is under new ownership, and dealing with termites, spiders, and leaks is the life-long process of sanctification. We spend our lives on earth endeavoring to become like Christ through the power of the Holy Spirit. Healing prayer can be an important tool in the process of sanctification and can be helpful in dealing with deep-seated issues or pain.

Back to the topic at hand: envy. This year has involved quite a bit of planting and uprooting in my heart. The Lord prompted me to make healing prayer appointments to pray through some issues that keep cropping up. Yesterday, I invited the two women praying for me on a tour of my black black heart. I confessed how deeply my heart is riddled with envy. Each new season, each new friendship, each new whatever presents an opportunity for me to envy and I am weary in my bones of it.

A wake up call that I needed to start dealing with this more seriously was when I started envying other babies. I envied babies who were really calm, letting their mom accomplish all sorts of super mom things. I envied babies who slept late in the morning (we are on month four of 5:00 a.m. wake ups, ugh). I envied babies who ate everything and babies who liked the car seat. At first, I didn't realize the insidious root of my little thoughts of, "Oh, I wish Penny would sleep in," or "I wish Penny wouldn't scream in the car most of the time so I could actually go places." But as I started unpacking these thoughts, their ugly origin became clear. Ahh! I was letting my propensity to envy invade my sweet relationship with my daughter. Not cool. Time to deal with it. I want to excise this emotion from my heart; I want it over and done.

You might meet me and think, "It's kind of weird this girl has such a thing with envy." I am not the saddest human you'll ever meet, and my life is pretty great. It's not even that I wish I could trade places with all the lives I envy. I don't want to trade places. I like my life, I like myself (most of the time), and I really like all my people. It's as if I want to pick and choose all the very best pieces of everyone else and collect them for myself. I want this house, that car, this skill or ability, that hair, those eyes, her skin, her legs, her body. On the inside, I believe yet another lie, "I am not good enough, and if I could have all of these things, I would be good enough and I would be permanently happy." The belief in this lie is truly, utterly ridiculous once I write it out in a sentence, but deep in my psyche, that's what it all boils down to. Yikes!

Back to healing prayer. As one woman was praying for me, she asked the Lord to strengthen me so that I would not continue breaking the Tenth Commandment. "You shall not covet your neighbor's house. You shall not covet your neighbor's wife, or his male or female servant, his ox or donkey, or anything that belongs to your neighbor" (Exodus 20:17).

Ten is usually a good number for me. My birthday is on the tenth. Ten days is the perfect length for a vacation (1 day for travel, 1 day to unwind, 6 days to play, 1 day for packing up and travel, and a sacred buffer day at home). It's a nice, even number and as the first double digit, it starts off the larger numbers with a quiet elegance. Ten people make a great dinner party, small enough to be intimate, yet large enough to feel festive.

Let's talk about what not's pretty or festive: breaking the Tenth

Commandment. I don't often think about the Ten Commandments, so I was surprised when they came up. Sheesh! Breaking the Tenth Commandment! There are only ten, surely I can keep it together enough to follow ten simple commandments? I realized that no, I can't do that at all, at least not on my own. I confessed, I repented, and I asked the Lord to help me grow, to give me spiritual tools to combat the temptation to covet. Because "he who promised is faithful," I am confident that the Lord will provide what I need to keep healing in this area (Hebrews 10:23 ESV).

Lie replacement therapy (using the truth of God to combat the lies of the enemy) is one of the most effective and powerful tools at our disposal when we're combating an invasion of our thought life. The following verses have been incredibly helpful for me to cling to and meditate on as the Lord rewires the envious pathways of my mind, leading me gently but firmly to a place of contentment. Matthew 6:19–25 says:

> Do not store up for yourselves treasures on earth, where moth and rust destroy, and where thieves break in and steal. But store up for yourselves treasures in heaven, where moth and rust do not destroy, and where thieves do not break in and steal. For where your treasure is, there your heart will be also.

> The eye is the lamp of the body. If your eyes are good, your whole body will be full of light. But if your eyes are bad, your whole body will be full of darkness. If then the light within you is darkness, how great is that darkness! No one can serve two masters. Either he will hate the one and love the other, or he will be devoted to the one and despise the other. You cannot serve both God and Money.

> Therefore I tell you, do not worry about your life,
> what you will eat or drink; or about your body, what
> you will wear. Is not life more important than food,
> and the body more important than clothes?

It's funny how you can read a verse or a passage a thousand times, but at just the right time, the Lord can bring it up again, making his Word real in a completely new way. This passage is well known, I'm sure I've heard more than one sermon about it, but somehow I've always thought about these verses separately. When you look at the passage as a whole, it's clear that Jesus has us pegged. He talks about our hearts, our eyes, and our worry. He knows us intimately; He knows how we're wired. He knows that everything begins with our hearts and our eyes. First, he admonishes us not to store up our treasures on earth. I've always thought about this passage with regard to not accumulating a bunch stuff that will rust out and break. (This verse really helped me when my puppy shredded the exquisite wedding shoes that were a special gift from my father.)

It's certainly important to check our consumerism, but it's deeper than that. This verse is getting at our hearts. Even if the house is empty, the car is on its last legs, and the clothes are worn and ragged, we can still be storing up our treasures on earth. I am good at storing up mounds of earthly treasure in my heart. I fantasize about my dream home. I daydream about new clothes. I fall asleep thinking about what I might look like if I tried that workout or got my hands on that miracle cream made of stardust and diamond bits.

I don't want to live there anymore. I want my mind and my heart and my outward trappings to reflect a heavenly focus, an eternal perspective. I'm not going to lie, I like nice stuff. With years of envy under my belt, I've got an eye for it. I can spot the good stuff a mile away, and every time I do, it pricks a little twinge in my heart. This brings us to the very next thing Jesus says in verse 22, "the eye is the lamp of the body," making all things good or bad. Envy begins with our eyes. We see, we take it in, and then it's all about what we choose to do next. We can launch into the pathways of envy and covetousness, or we can begin the discipline of pursuing contentment with the help of the Holy Spirit.

Even Peter, the rock upon whom God would build his church, struggled with envy. In John 21, Jesus asks Peter three times if he loves him. Hurt and probably a little exasperated, Peter says, "Lord, you know all things; you know that I love you." Then Jesus gives Peter instructions to "Feed my sheep," and warns Peter that an unpleasant death awaits him. Jesus concludes by saying, "Follow me!"

As Peter is taking this in, he notices that John, the disciple whom Jesus loved, is following them. Eager to know what fate awaits John, Peter says, in essence, "But Jesus, what about him? Will he die a terrible death too?" Jesus answers, "If I want him to remain alive until I return, what is that to you? You must follow me" (John 21:17–22). Peter's heart is catching the first whiff of envy. He's wondering, will John die a terrible death like me? What are you doing with him, Lord? Maybe I'd prefer what you're doing with John instead of your plan for me? If I'm going to go through this, I want to make sure he is too. Or, I at least want to know what you're planning to do with him so I can weigh the scales. But Jesus knows where this line of thinking leads. Jesus keys in on exactly what Peter (and what we, thousands of years later) need to hear: "It doesn't matter what I'm doing with him, it matters what I'm doing with you. You must follow me."

C.S. Lewis captures this perpetual exchange with Jesus perfectly in *The Horse and His Boy* when Aslan (a lion symbolizing Jesus) is explaining how he's been present throughout the life of the boy, Shasta. Shasta listens to Aslan, but becomes distracted by the story of his friend Aravis. He wants to know why Aslan chose to wound her. In a gentle rebuke, Aslan says:

"I was the lion." And as Shasta gaped with open mouth and said nothing, the Voice continued. "I was the lion who forced you to join with Aravis. I was the cat who comforted you among the houses of the dead. I was the lion who drove the jackals from you while you slept. I was the lion who gave the Horses the new strength of fear for the last mile so that you should reach King Lune in time. And I was the lion you do not remember who pushed the boat in which you lay, a child near death, so that it came to shore where a man sat, wakeful at midnight, to receive you."

"Then it was you who wounded Aravis?"

"It was I"

"But what for?"

"Child," said the Voice, "I am telling you your story, not hers. I tell no one any story but his own."[9]

He only tells us our own story. He wants us to focus on our love story with him. He's asking us to be diligent, content, and faithful in the exact and specific work he has given us to do. He wants us to stop looking to the right or the left at what everybody else is doing.

Jesus intimately knows the battle raging in our hearts. He knows the competition between the flesh and the spirit. When he was tempted in the desert, he was offered food after fasting for 40 days. He was offered power and splendor, but he resisted temptation, responding to Satan with the truth of Scripture (Matthew 4:1–10). He knew that he could not both fulfill his calling and indulge in

---

9   Lewis, C.S. *The Horse and His Boy.* New York: Harper Collins, 1954.

Satan's temptation. Similarly, we "cannot serve two masters," we will "hate the one and love the other" (Matthew 6:24). We have to choose who we will serve, both once (justification) and every day (sanctification).

He calls us to a higher way of living, to be content in a striving world. We are invited to be at peace in a world full of worry. So much of our time is taken up with exactly what Jesus tells us not to worry about—our lives, what we eat, and what we wear. From the moment we wake up to the moment we go to bed, we are contemplating our needs and worrying about how to meet them. Jesus woos us with freedom, drawing us in with a simple "Do not worry." Do not worry about your life; I have it all in hand. Do not worry about your sustenance; I will feed you. Do not worry about your garments; I will clothe you. His exhortation to cease worrying is accompanied by a concrete assurance that he will meet all our needs. Jesus doesn't tell us to run around stark naked and starving because he wants us to pretend we're not human. He's not asking us to stop caring about all the physical things that affect us on a daily basis. What he is saying is *don't worry* about these things for "your heavenly Father knows that you need them."

I want Jesus to be the Lord and Master of my heart, my eyes, and my worry. Envy leaves me empty, striving, and poor. I'm kicking it to the curb. I'm focusing on what God is saying in my story. I want to store up my treasures (even in my mind) in heaven, because that is where I want my heart. I want to be at peace in a worry-filled world. Most of all, I want my heart up there with Jesus, eternally content at his side.

The Eye is the Lamp of the Body

> The eye is the lamp of the body. If your eyes are
> healthy, your whole body will be full of light.
> (Matthew 6:22).

> Finally, brothers and sisters, whatever is true,
> whatever is noble, whatever is right, whatever is
> pure, whatever is lovely, whatever is admirable—if
> anything is excellent or praiseworthy—think about
> such things. (Philippians 4:8)

Previously, I wrote to you about envy and the Lord's grace in revealing my propensity to engage in this sin. In the healing prayer appointment I referenced, we also talked about how my heart came to be this way. Sometimes it's possible to pinpoint habits, practices, or moments that begin a pattern of habituated sin. I can't recall the exact moment when I let envy take up residence, but if I had to pinpoint the root of this sin, I'd say my relationship to media played a big role.

As a teenager, I devoured beauty and celebrity magazines. I was always trying to get my hands on them, carefully poring over each picture, each dress, each photomontage of "Stars are just like Us!" As a young girl, I lacked the spiritual and emotional maturity to filter these images. I let the root of envy in through images of perfection, reading about beauty treatments and creams, hair color and gorgeous clothes. I thought, "If I just have that eye cream, or if I just try that hair color, or if I follow this diet for a week, or buy those pants, then I will be beautiful enough." Fashion, beauty, and lovely clothes are not, in and of themselves, bad things, but they are easily manipulable. I lacked the discernment to enjoy the good parts and leave the rest. I took it all in, hook, line, and sinker.

Maybe someday I can revisit those fun magazines with a more discerning eye (who doesn't love a big fat *InStyle* magazine?), but for right now, I'm taking a break because I'm not ready for it yet. I'm also trying to spend most of my free time reading or doing other things (You might still catch me at the airport or the nail salon catching up on the Oscar dresses!).

I am also a voracious reader. I love to get lost in a story. The pure escapism of an engrossing novel has been my siren call since I was a little girl. In fact, I can vividly remember the first Saturday I spent the curled up in my parents' bed reading the entire day away. Even now, my idea of a perfect Saturday involves sleeping in, staying in bed until late in the afternoon, drinking coffee, and reading a great novel. A love of reading is a wondrous gift, an immediate transport from the doctor's office waiting room to an adventure in a foreign land.

The characters in a well-told story become my friends and companions. I give myself to them with my whole heart, and I mourn the loss of their friendship when the story is over. I often wait a long time before finishing the final book in a series or the last season of a show I've loved, because then it's not really over. I can imagine the story continuing and the characters going on with their lives because I haven't experienced the end.

Over the last few years, the Lord has been so kind in showing me the need for discernment regarding my media consumption. I'm incredibly sensitive to books, movies, and even the newspaper. I cannot watch things other people can watch and remain unaffected. The story infiltrates my mind, taking up residence in my soul. I can't watch scary movies or tolerate violence because I'll have nightmares for weeks. I hate watching stories about marriages falling apart or infidelity because I internalize the situation and begin to worry it will happen to me.

Growing up, we seldom watched TV and didn't even have one for a few years. Since my personality has two speeds, "on" or "off," I have a pretty addictive relationship to TV when it's available to me. My husband and I have been married for seven years, but we've never had cable, and only briefly had a television that could be used to watch DVDs. But don't you worry, I still got my binge-watching accomplished through the miracle of internet streaming. For someone who doesn't have a TV, it's pretty amazing how much I manage to watch TV.

It's been a slow process of weeding out particular elements of media, but the Lord has been very gracious and tender as he's asked me to give up certain things. It was a long time before I was even ready to start having these conversations with him. As a result of this process, we have streamlined our media consumption, limiting both content and which days of the week we watch. I have learned the hard way that I have to be more careful with media than other people I know. Because I know this about myself, I don't want to be overly prescriptive in discussing media consumption. Media consumption might look different for people at various times in their lives. Right after I had Penny, all our media consumption guidelines went out the window and my inner binge-watcher feasted on TV during the day while nursing. There have also been times when my media consumption has not reflected the values I espouse as a Christian. Yet the Lord stuck with me in those times, gently asking me to give up things I loved to watch and read, but replacing them with better, more beautiful stories and images.

Recently, a woman in our church spoke about entertainment and discipleship, sharing from her own journey of wrestling with her relationship to media. What I liked most about the sermon was the fact that she wasn't definitive about what we should and shouldn't be watching. Instead, she encouraged the congregation to be thoughtful, introspective, and inquisitive about media.

I think that's just the right tack. If we launch into creating a blacklist and an approved list, our efforts will soon be derailed and we will have neglected the heart of the matter. Instead, I want to encourage you to be thoughtful and prayerful about this area of your life. Media is everywhere in our culture, you cannot escape it. Its ubiquity is probably Satan's greatest advantage because we don't even think about it anymore. If there's any fertile breeding ground for the enemy, it's an area of our lives we don't think worthy of prayerful consideration. The phrase, "You are what you eat" applies equally to our eyes. You are what you see. What we take in with our eyes becomes part of who we are, whether or not we make a conscious decision. The images, stories, and characters are filed away, sometimes forever, in our mental rolodex. The eye is truly the lamp of the body. Our eyes let in light or they let in darkness. We cannot afford to let what we take in with our eyes go unexamined.

Sanctification, our lifelong process of becoming like Christ, involves regular 360 degree scans of our minds and hearts, including our media consumption. Regularly ask yourself, what's going on in my life? What am I consuming and why? How is my relationship to media affecting my heart? What would Jesus think about this? How do I feel after watching this? Was it edifying? Was it worthy of my time and emotional energy? What else could I be doing with my time? Is my media consumption reflecting appropriate leisure time or am I zoning out to delay dealing with deeper issues?

Media consumption is a tough area. I believe consumption even extends to the amount of time we spend looking at our phones and social media. The temptations of unhealthy media are scintillating, titillating, beautiful, and hilarious (hilarity is my Achilles heel). But we don't have to walk this tightrope alone and I don't think there are always clear cut right and wrong answers. Fortunately, Jesus wants to be present in our media choices. He wants to be part of the conversation, and he wants us to walk with the Holy Spirit as guide for our eyes and our hearts. I also think Jesus probably appreciates a really hilarious episode, a glossy spread of exquisitely designed gowns, or an utterly absorbing novel. As you invite the Lord into your media choices, my prayer for you is that you would be wise as serpents and innocent as doves. "Behold, I am sending you out as sheep in the midst of wolves, so be wise as serpents and innocent as doves" (Matthew 10:16 ESV).

Remain Steadfast.

I Will Become Even More Undignified

I will celebrate before the Lord. I will become even more undignified than this... (2 Samuel 6:21–22)

Praise the Lord, all you nations; extol him, all you peoples.
For great is his love toward us, and the faithfulness of the Lord endures forever. (Psalm 117:1–2)

She has done a beautiful thing to me. (Mark 14:6)

Therefore, in view of God's mercy, offer your bodies as living sacrifices, holy and pleasing to God—for this is your spiritual act of worship. (Romans 12:1)

It's Holy Week. I love this week of eager anticipation, of yearning for deliverance, of sorrow redeemed by joy, and affliction healed by hope. On earth, we go all out to celebrate the birth of Jesus at Christmas, but oddly, Easter celebrations are a little more subdued. But I bet there's a huge party in heaven during Easter week! As we prepare our hearts and minds each year to contemplate the sorrow of the cross and the exultation of the resurrection, maybe heaven is also getting ready for a fantastical celebration? I'm sure celestial party planning far outshines prepping a ham and dying Easter eggs.

My Easter prayer for you is that the Holy Spirit fills you with a wriggly, elated expectancy. I hope you walk with a buoyant confidence in the goodness of God coupled with the quiet sensitivity to hear his whispers to your heart. Perhaps you have been fasting this Lenten season, creating space and time to listen, redirecting the prick of longing for chocolate or a stiff drink to focus on the Father. May the fruitfulness of this season abound long after Easter has come and gone.

Earlier this year, I was talking to two women in our church, both of whom I respect enormously. They are a few years older, with lots of children, experience, and hard-won wisdom. They shared how they love to see their children dance before the Lord, and often join in to dance together in worship, praising the Heavenly Father.

I thought, "Huh, that sounds like a good idea, maybe I'll try it sometime." The last few weeks I've been crying out to the Lord regarding some big career and location decisions in our life, and I finally started practicing this joyful discipline of unguarded worship. Don't get me wrong, I love to worship, and I'll definitely raise my hands in church, but you won't find me interpretative dancing in the aisles.

A certain worship song has been on repeat in our house for the last month, and here's what I've been doing: I put Penny down for a nap (she likes to dance with me too, but it usually results in some serious spit up, so we'll try it a little later), then I close all the blinds, turn up the speaker, and I dance wildly in my kitchen before the Lord, barefoot, singing at the top of my lungs with my not-for-public-consumption voice, and my never-to-be-seen-by-anyone-ever dancing.

I lift my hands in praise and I pray. As I lift up each person on my prayer list, I raise my arms really high, imagining I'm in the throne room of heaven, saying, "Here they are, Lord, do you see them? They really need you on this one, can you please work on this?" It's utterly intoxicating. It's freeing and gorgeous and I highly recommend the practice. Worship changes the character of the atmosphere, sanctifying the air, banishing the enemy, restoring our relationship with God.

In 2 Samuel 6, David brings the Ark of the Covenant to Jerusalem with a huge procession. The procession stops every five minutes to offer sacrifices. There's music, jubilant praise, but most of all, dancing before the Lord. The passage says David, "danced before the Lord with all His might." When David returned to the palace, his wife mocked him; she watched him dancing from the window, and "despised him in her heart" (2 Samuel 6:16).

His reply to her attempt to quell his fervor and stifle his joy is beautiful. His response should be the posture of our hearts at all times, "I will become even more undignified than this, and I will be humiliated in my own eyes." That's how I want to worship—bold and unafraid, undignified and silly, glorifying the Lord with the contents of my heart rather than the polish of my moves or the tenor of my voice.

In Mark 14, Jesus and the disciples are at the home of Simon the Leper in Bethany. Jesus will be arrested and crucified in a matter of days, but no one except Jesus has any inkling of what is to come. A woman enters their gathering with an alabaster jar of expensive perfume. She breaks the jar and pours it on his head as an act of worship. It's lavish and unnecessary. Anointing his head with perfume doesn't serve a purpose or prove a point; it's just a gift, a tangible act of worship for the King. When the disciples grumble about the cost, Jesus shushes them, saying, "She has done a beautiful thing to me."

I want my worship to be a beautiful thing to Jesus. I want to bless him with my praise. Maybe one way I can offer my body up as a living sacrifice, holy and pleasing to God, is to dance before him, bare and unashamed.

If You See Something, Say Something

When he arrived and saw the evidence of the grace of God, he was glad and encouraged them all to remain true to the Lord with all their hearts. (Acts 11:23)

I just got Penny down for a nap and my mind is going in a thousand different directions about what I should do with my precious time. Should I write? Should I clean? Should I prep dinner? Should I do work emails? I find that writing usually goes better in the morning, so I try to do that after my devotions if there's time. During the afternoon, I try to get things done around the house or work a little. A lot of times I just stare at the wall because that's what I need to do.

Whatever the few precious moments of quiet look like, I always give myself the first fifteen minutes of every nap to run around the house like a crazy person, picking things up, doing the breakfast dishes, switching the laundry, etc., so I can get a little order going in the chaos. It settles me to get a few things out of the way, but I have to give myself a time limit or I will suddenly find an hour gone as I'm completely absorbed in removing the window screens to wipe out the nasty window ledges that I never cared about until just this moment. Before I know it, she's up and I've done nothing important. So fifteen minutes, and that's it. Ok, sometimes I cheat and it's thirty minutes, but the concept is sound.

Today, I planned to knock out a few emails, but a quick peek in the mailbox sealed the deal that writing was the order of the day because I've been meaning to write about this topic for months now. As I reached down to manhandle the stacks of unsolicited magazines we receive (how did you find me Hannah Anderson and why do I want to give you all my money?), a cheery pink card peeked out and I thought, "Yes! Real mail!"

The outside bore my friend Bex's lovely script and I thought, "Mmm, haven't done anything lately to deserve a thank-you note, I wonder what this is." Inside was a *beautiful* Mother's Day card and a letter that brought me to tears. I'm not her mom; I'm just her friend. But she sent me a Mother's Day card just because. She said she was proud of me and happy to do life together, and she encouraged me to keep writing. It was just what I needed; I will live off that encouragement for weeks. A kind word from a good friend will defeat a thousand critics.

And Bex is a good friend. Our lives have been almost completely parallel since we both moved to DC about eight years ago. We got married within a month of each other, we bought houses at the same time and four blocks apart, we endured a grueling three years of law school together and she's the only reason I didn't throw in the towel. Last year, we both gave birth to baby girls ten weeks apart. We have walked through each of these major transitions side by side, holding hands, gripping elbows, or squeezing tight, whatever the occasion required.

Our lives are about to shift and it makes me sad to think that we will probably have our second babies in different cities and may never live in the same place again. She's moving abroad next summer for her husband's job, so I am a little bit excited to have multiple reasons to visit Europe: friends, cheese, wine, cheese and wine. Oh and art, I guess.

It's a rare and beautiful thing when someone pauses to say how much they love you or takes the time to put words to the fruit they see in your life. Acknowledging the effort, applauding the success, and encouraging through the tough spots—that is true friendship. I have been immeasurably blessed to know and love a group of women who speak life into my darkest corners. The gift of their friendship is on the short list of my most treasured blessings. I *need* my ladies. The Lord has given me some really good ones, so I want to make sure they know how much I care about them.

This is where the phrase, "If you see something, say something," comes in handy. You may be familiar with this catchy slogan in the context of terrorism alerts, as in, "If you see a super sketchy situation going down, say something." It's most certainly a good idea as it pertains to our national security, but it's also very useful in the context of loving others well.

A few years ago, a gentleman in our church spoke at the men's prayer breakfast using this phrase as his title, and when Pete came home and told me about it, the concept stuck with me. He told the men to speak life, and speak it often. He exhorted them to encourage their teams at work and tell their wives they're beautiful on every possible occasion. He said that every time your kids do something that makes your heart ache with love for them, tell them so. You can't go wrong speaking life into the people you love; it's a winning proposition. Take that, terrorists.

Around this same time, we went to a going away party for a friend. This going away party blew my socks off. Seriously, every single person who spoke said the kindest, most wonderfully adoring things about this woman. There were original song tributes, poetry, and themed food. It was nuts in the best possible way. At that time, I was still deeply struggling with envy, so of course, I left thinking, "I wish I were like that. I wish people would say those nice things about me. They probably wouldn't. Whomp. Whomp." But God was doing his work in me, and a glimmer of goodness made its way through the envy. I left that night thinking, "This was a great farewell party, but what if everyone had said those things to her *while she still lived here*." That way, she could feel awesome and loved and actually spend time with the people who think she's great instead of getting on a plane the next day to move away.

Since then, I've been trying to make "If you see something, say something" my personal mantra. I encourage you to make it yours. Now, we shouldn't just go around passing out plentiful but insincere compliments. It's only worth saying something if you actually see something. I'm sure most of you are great at noticing the good in others since you're probably a lovely person. I'm trying to make a point of saying all the nice things I think about people out loud. This means I have a lot of conversations with strangers about their shoes or their bag or their trench coat. I am that awkward girl. I try to limit it to two compliments because Bex, being the excellent friend that she is, informed me that after that it gets weird. Having recently been on the receiving end of a weird stranger compliment situation, I now agree with her. My apologies to all the stylishly dressed girls in DC I have weirded out on the sidewalk.

Superficial compliments are nice but character compliments are even better. They show you know somebody; they show you care enough to observe. It's nice to be told you're pretty but it's even better to be told you're kind. And it's awesome when someone notices the character traits or features that make you uniquely you.

I am absolutely positive that a thousand wonderful thoughts about other people occur to each one of you every day. SAY. THEM. OUT. LOUD. Just try it for one week! You won't turn back.

Quick to Listen, Slow to Speak

Even fools are thought wise if they keep silent, and discerning if they hold their tongues. (Proverbs 17:28)

We know that we all possess knowledge. Knowledge puffs up, but love builds up. The man who thinks he knows something does not yet know as he ought to know. But the man who loves God is known by God. (1 Corinthians 8:1–3)

Quick to listen, slow to speak, slow to become angry. (James 1:19)

I have two friends this week who are heading into tricky situations. They are preparing to spend time with people where the slightest spark could ignite a powder keg of emotion. Hurt, anger, frustration, perceived slights, and power plays ripple beneath the surface of every conversation. The tiniest shift could mean an eruption of saying things that are better left unsaid.

These two women know what they're up against, and they wisely asked for prayer covering. As I've been praying for them, it occurred to me that we spend a lot of time thinking, preparing, and praying about what we are going to say, but hardly any time at all thinking, preparing, and praying about *what we are not going to say.*

When preparing for a big presentation or a speech in front of a room full of people, you spend weeks thinking about just the right thing to say. You order your thoughts, draft an outline, and maybe even rehearse in front of the mirror. That time and thought is necessary for success. As my mom likes to say, "Success is when preparation meets opportunity." If you didn't prepare, you'd be nervous, anxious, and you might make a fool of yourself. You could end up being a YouTube viral sensation, and not in a good way.

What if when we're headed into a tricky meeting or a potentially stressful weekend, we spent time asking the Lord for wisdom about when to speak and when to remain silent? If you grew up with this adage drilled into you, "If you can't say anything nice, don't say anything at all," perhaps you're already a pro in this area. But if you're like me, then you could use some more practice. In my family of origin, our motto is "No unexpressed thought or emotion." I come from a family of talkers and usually, it's pretty great. We get it all out there; we talk about hard, uncomfortable things. But there is a time for wisdom; there is a time for restraint.

I have all sorts of ideas and opinions about how other people should handle things. In another life, I should have been a life coach. I would love to tell people what to do *and* have them pay me for it. (And then you could all mock me mercilessly behind my back, secretly thinking, "Life coach? Not a thing.") True life confession: one day, during those dark months post-law school graduation, I had fake business cards made for my imaginary life coaching business just to cheer myself up. I found them the other day while cleaning out a drawer and they made me smile. The cards had a cheesy slogan to the effect of "Your life just got better," and my name and email address. If you're feeling super down, try making yourself business cards for your dream job and keep them lying around. In a few months or years, maybe they can be your real business cards. Or, if you're like me, the Lord might take you in a completely different (and better) direction than you ever could have imagined.

Being an attorney is sort of like being a life coach, except you tell people how to comply with complicated statutory obligations or how to structure businesses to avoid tax liabilities. Not as sexy, right? I'd much rather advise someone on starting a new fitness plan or how to pack the perfect capsule collection for traveling abroad.

Back to keeping our mouths shut. When emotions are running high, it's time for some serious introspection. You gotta check yourself before you wreck yourself. If you know in your heart that you can't say anything nice if a certain topic comes up, I'd like to suggest taking a knee.

Get on your knees before the Lord and ask him to guard your tongue. Ask him for discernment about what to say and when to say it. Most importantly, ask him for the diligence and strength to remain silent when it's best to do so. This will be especially hard when your defenses are raised. It's so easy to take the bait when we already feel injured or wronged. I don't know about you, but I desperately want to be right. I love being right. I am convinced I'm right almost 100% of the time. I will belabor a point for hours just to prove I'm right. I will beat a dead horse into the ground if it will make my case.

But what happens when I'm right yet it destroys the relationship? What happens when I'm right but I've failed to show love or extend grace? I become like "a resounding gong or a clanging cymbal" (1 Corinthians 13:1).

That's why I love this word from 1 Corinthians 8:1–3:

> We know that we all possess knowledge. Knowledge puffs up, but love builds up. The man who thinks he

knows something does not yet know as he ought to
know. But the man who loves God is known by God.

In this section, Paul is discussing the consumption of food
sacrificed to idols, and admonishing believers not to consume such
food items if it will cause other believers to stumble. In essence, he's
saying, "Guys, you and I both know that eating food sacrificed to
idols isn't a big deal because we're under the new covenant. But your
brothers and sisters who have recently converted to Christianity
after a lifetime of idol worship are struggling with it. How about we
all cool it on the debate, and instead extend grace? Why don't you
drop the issue of being right or wrong, and start thinking about how
you can help them in their walk with the Lord?"

Whoa. That's a totally different perspective. If we leave the "You
should haves," and the "I want tos," and the "But that was wrongs,"
behind, we can begin the holy practice of extending grace. Sure,
knowledge can puff us up; being right feels good. But what does love
do? It *builds up*. I want to build others up with my words and deeds. I
want to build others up with my silence. I want to be "quick to listen,
slow to speak, and slow to become angry" (James 1:19).

Somewhere I read about asking yourself three questions before
you speak: (1) Is it truthful? (2) Is it kind? (3) Did they ask for my
opinion? If I diligently practiced asking these questions, I think you
would find me a lot less loquacious!

So how do we begin this process? Because the Holy Spirit
dwells in us, we have all wisdom, knowledge, and discernment at
our fingertips. But we need to learn how to seek the Lord and *listen*
to his prompting. Scripture says he speaks in a still, small voice (1
Kings 19:12). Start putting the time in to ask the Lord about when
to remain silent. When you're heading into a dicey situation, try
spending just as much time asking the Lord to restrain your tongue
as you do asking him to give you the words to say.

I would be remiss if I didn't address what to do with all those unsaid thoughts and feelings, although the solution isn't rocket science (it's pretty much the panacea for everything). Even if we don't voice our grievances, they're still rolling around in our heads, bumping up against our will and self-control, vying for attention. It's really important that we don't let our unexpressed emotions become roots of bitterness in our hearts. If we choose to nurse a grudge rather than address an issue through conversation, we've just shifted the problem. We will become heavy laden with all the burdens and grudges and slights. You're probably thinking, "So what am I supposed to do? Just pretend they don't exist?"

No. We're going to take them to the foot of the cross where they belong. Jesus tells us, "My yoke is easy and my burden is light" (Matthew 11:30). He can handle our wild and angry thoughts. In fact, he specializes in them. Bring them to the author and perfecter of our faith. Then revel in the silence. See what happens when you prepare your heart to take your grievances to him rather than out on other people.

He Stood in Awe of My Name

> My covenant was with him, a covenant of life and peace, and I gave them to him; this called for reverence and he revered me and stood in awe of my name. True instruction was in his mouth and nothing false was found on his lips. He walked with me in peace and uprightness, and turned many from sin. (Malachi 2:5–6)

It's another 4:50 a.m. wake-up morning and I am lagging! I've been trying a new routine of waking up before Penny in order to have some semblance of sanity for the day. But it's just rough. I can't seem to get my head around it. I'm pounding some strong black tea and writing to you instead of lying facedown on my couch, which is what I really want to do right now.

I've been thinking a lot about how irreplaceably unique the family unit is designed to be, particularly the relationship between husband and wife. I am the only witness to the daily intimacies of Pete's life and he is the only witness to mine. We share a home, a bed, a child, a life together. Besides his parents, there is no one on earth more intimately acquainted with him than I am. With that privilege comes great responsibility.

Praying for your husband or other people you are in close-relationship with is important. Lately I've been praying this passage in Malachi over my husband, but everyone can benefit from praying through Malachi 2:5–6:

> My covenant was with him, a covenant of life and peace, and I gave them to him; this called for reverence and he revered me and stood in awe of my name. True instruction was in his mouth and nothing false was found on his lips. He walked with me in peace and uprightness, and turned many from sin.

The Lord has been impressing upon me the importance of praying for my husband fervently, frequently, and fastidiously. If I'm not praying for him, who is? I am his spiritual wingman, I need to give him prayer cover, and there is nobody better situated than I am to see the weak spots and vulnerabilities. Rather than making weak spots, vulnerabilities, and flaws a source of contention, I'm trying to pray into them instead. I also regularly ask the Lord to bless him, to help him grow, to strengthen and encourage him, and to give him favor before God and men.

"He revered [God] and stood in awe of his name"

A few months ago I came across this beautiful gem of a passage at the very end of the Old Testament. It's in Malachi, one of the minor prophets, and the verses fall in the middle of a chapter containing an admonition for the priests. Malachi is exhorting the priests to emulate the righteousness of their ancestor, Levi, the father of the Levites, the priestly tribe that served God in the tabernacle and the temple.

As I was reading this description of Levi, these verses jumped out at me as a powerful way to pray for the men in my life. God made a covenant of life and peace with Levi, and God says, "and I gave them to him." The Lord promised Levi life and peace, and he fulfilled his promise. The gifts of life and peace called for reverence from Levi, and "he revered me and stood in awe of my name." Levi revered the Lord and stood in awe of him. I am praying that God would grant Pete life and peace. I'm asking that Pete would see the hand of God at work in his life and revere God, standing in awe of his name.

Let me tell you something, there is no greater gift than a godly husband. Sure, it's nice if Pete loves me, and it's nice if he loves our kids. But you know what I care about more than anything? I care that he *loves* the Lord and is *listening to his voice*. If my husband is following hard after God, everything else will go a whole lot better.

A godly man is filled daily with God's love for others. He's operating out of a place of provision from the Lord. He's not left exclusively to his fallen human nature to meet the demands we place upon him. A godly man has strength, grace, and love at his fingertips through the constant provision of the Holy Spirit. I don't know about you, but there are a lot of days when I haven't done anything to deserve Pete's love, but he chooses to love me because he serves a higher master than just our marriage. His love for me is part of a covenant he made before God, so he chooses love and forgiveness when it would be easier to shut down or withdraw. Earthly love is fleeting, difficult to satisfy, and hard to keep. But love from a man who reveres God and stands in awe of him is of a totally different nature. I want to be loved by a man who loves God first and foremost.

"True instruction was in his mouth and nothing false was found on his lips"

I am praying that the Lord would equip Pete to instruct others in wisdom and truth. It's not easy to tell the truth. A little white lie here, a tiny omission there, and quickly our mouths become sullied with lies. I like this imagery, "true instruction was in his mouth." It's vivid—the words of truth are rolling around in his mouth, ready to be poured out in wisdom and love. We can't have true instruction in our mouths unless we have the Word of God deeply rooted in our hearts. I'm praying for the Lord to give Pete a hunger for his Word. I am asking the Lord to keep Pete's heart pure, and as a result, that nothing false would be found on his lips. I'm asking that Pete would speak truth and maintain integrity.

"He walked with me in peace and uprightness"

It is a gift to be in the presence of peaceful person. You can sense their serenity; their poise quiets the room. There's no better combination than a peaceful person who walks with the Lord. I am asking the Lord to walk with Pete in peace, to quiet his anxious heart, and to give him peace that surpasses understanding. As for uprightness, I am asking the Lord to make him above reproach, to convict him through the Holy Spirit when necessary, and to guide his steps into righteousness.

"And turned many from sin"

I want my husband to turn me from sin. I want him to turn our children from sin. Through example, love, encouragement, exhortation, and, if necessary, confrontation, I want Pete to be the kind of man who turns many from sin, so I'm asking the Lord to continue shaping his character and to use him mightily.

I encourage you to pray for your families. Lift them up before the Lord, cover them with your prayers. My prayer is that as you pray, you begin to see his faithfulness in specific, miraculous ways.

What Are You Waiting For?

Behold, You have made my days as [short as] hand widths, and my lifetime is as nothing in Your sight. Surely every man at his best is a mere breath [a wisp of smoke, a vapor that vanishes]! (Psalm 39:5 AMP)

A person can do nothing better than to eat and drink and find satisfaction in their own toil. This too, I see, is from the hand of God, for without him, who can eat or find enjoyment? (Ecclesiastes 2:24–25)

Recently, we had the opportunity to get away to The Homestead for two nights for the first time since Penny was born. The Homestead is a magical resort about three and a half hours outside of DC. Built in 1766 by Thomas Bullitt, a contemporary of George Washington, it is a national treasure. The property has passed through many hands over the years, but its epicurean spirit of serenity remains intact. It's stunningly beautiful, quiet, and best of all, totally luxurious without being pretentious. Our time there was heaven. We ate, slept, hiked, talked, enjoyed fishing and massages, and savored every second of it. While reminiscing over the past decade together, I said I wouldn't change anything about the last ten years except my attitude. Thinking back on our early years, without a mortgage, or a child, or the obligations that inevitably accompany growing older, I wish I could go back and shake myself. I'd say, "Get out of that funk! This is great! You have no responsibilities! Sleep in! Stay up late! Go dancing!"

Instead of waking up to an unscheduled weekend and wondering, a la Mindy Kaling, "Is everyone hanging out without me?" I should have said, "Yes! This is fantastic! Let's go hiking in the Shenandoah." Wallowing in regret is not a place the Lord asks us to dwell, but it is often an instructive and useful place to visit once in a while. Now that the moments of free time I used to take for granted are precious and rare, my attitude is markedly improved. I'm hoping this new attitude makes its way deep into my heart.

I've been thinking a lot about the question, what are you waiting for? For a long time, my answer had been, "I'm waiting for the next thing." I'm yearning for what's beyond. I want to get to the place where the big questions plaguing me right now are answered. I want to live at the exact point in time when I will experience certainty about all the things that make me uneasy. I want to fast forward to the time when everything will be good. One day. Some day.

Newsflash! That place? That day? It doesn't exist this side of eternity. When I was little, I wanted so badly to be a grown-up, to be my own boss, to be in love, to be married, to have a job, to be in the next phase. I wasn't unhappy or terribly distraught (usually), but longing for the future was a constant undercurrent in my thoughts. My daydreams involved a nice car and beautiful homes because my childhood dream was to be a realtor. I guess I wanted to be a realtor because we visited lots of open houses on the weekends?

Oh how many hours I wasted, wishing and hoping for the future because I fantasized that things would be different, better. But it's the times in between that make up most of our days. The now and not yet are fundamental to human existence.

The truth is the tiny moments matter. The days when nothing

big happened, when nothing meaningful was accomplished, they matter. Those days make up ninety-percent of our lives. Why am I always wishing them away, waiting for the next big thing and chasing some imagined high?

On Monday, I was talking to a dear friend who recently suffered the loss of a beloved grandparent. I was sad and a little angry on her behalf. She is just exiting a long season of waiting and heartache. It's only been a few weeks since the Lord graciously and lavishly took her out of the desert with a glorious answer to prayer. I wanted more time for her to be happy. My first instinct was one of spiritual immaturity as I said, "Ugh, I'm so sad and mad for you, you just got this amazing news and now you're sad again. I feel like you deserved to be happier longer."

She was kind and wise as she gently shared, "Natalie, that's not life. It's never going to be like that. It will always be a mix of the good and the bad; we live in a fallen world. When I feel sadness or experience hardship, I'm trying to make a point of finding blessings, even little ones, to remind me of the goodness of God."

You might be thinking, "Duh, Natalie, don't you know that it won't all be good by now?" And I do, I do know that, but what I haven't kicked yet is the *yearning* for everything to be good and exciting. Maybe that's why I've spent so much of my life trying to jab the fast forward button on the remote control of my mind. But we need to take the good with the bad, the exciting with the mundane. For the most part, the mundane and the bad are not just seasons to "get through" or "grin and bear it." I don't want to spend the majority of my life just "getting through." Who wants to do that?

When I read inspirational articles or meet people doing exciting, world-changing things, I'm tempted to entertain grandiose ambitions swiftly followed by discouragement as I remember that my time is accounted for and my life is pretty ordinary. When some awesome Ted Talk person looks into the camera after solving the world hunger problem in less than twenty minutes and says, "What are you waiting for?" I think, "Yes! I should do something important! I should go be awesome!" Cue the inspirational montage from Sister Act where Whoopi Goldberg leads the nuns into the gritty neighborhood, transforming it with paint, flowers, and hugs in the span of three action-packed minutes.

If only we could get our own inspirational fast-forward montage to get us through the painstaking hard work of grown-up life. Alas, that fast forward button only exists in movies. As mere mortals, we have to live every waking hour of every day. Whether it's the middle of the night or the longest hours of the day, (after second nap but before Pete gets home) if you're awake, you have two choices. You can choose to be present, to really inhabit your life, or you can choose to check out and mentally push fast forward.

Lately, the Lord is inviting me to be fully present in my life. He is inviting me to soak it all in, to stay here a while, to hold the now and not yets in tension, acknowledging their existence but not letting them overwhelm my spirit. I'm working on my answer to the question, "What are you waiting for?" Instead of saying, "Everything," the answer is beginning to be, "Nothing." I'm not waiting for anything.

He has given me this lovely life, this marvelous family to love day in, day out. The long walks, the early mornings, the tender snuggles, the slobbery kisses, the loads and loads of laundry, the perpetual dishes, *this is my life*. And I am not waiting for anything else. Our lives are made in the quiet corners, in the faithful pursuit of the ordinary obligations of being human.

As the Lord is asking me to be present, I'm trying to say yes. I don't want to wish my whole life away yearning for the highs. A few weeks ago, I was walking with Penny and Sam in Congressional Cemetery. It was the perfect time of day, the sun streaming through blossoming trees. Sam was backlit as he frolicked among the ancient gravestones. The grass glowed a brilliant green and Penny kicked her feet in delight, cooing at Sam's antics. I was praying, thanking God for the moment, but also, you guessed it, asking about what's next for us. He gave me two words, "Work and relish." Do the work I've given you. Relish your life.

He has given me tangible work to do right here, right now. He has given me a gorgeous life filled with good friends, ordinary days, and his extraordinary grace. I'm relishing it.

Be At Rest Once More

I am still confident of this: I will see the goodness
of the Lord in the land of the living. Wait for the
Lord; be strong and take heart and wait for the
Lord. (Psalm 27:13–14)

Be at rest once more, O my soul, for the Lord has
been good to you. For you, O lord, have delivered
my soul from death, my eyes from tears, my feet
from stumbling, that I may walk before the Lord in
the land of the living. (Psalm 116:7–9)

I am writing to you while snuggled up in a big king bed with
piles of pillows perched behind me, a glittering lake winking at me
through the window, and an adorable husband gently snoozing in
his ikat-printed eye mask (a gift from my mom for his recent trip to
Korea). I was shocked this morning when I rolled over to find him
still asleep beside me since I don't think we've both slept in past
6:00 a.m. in ages. Bless my parents who took the morning stretch
with our committed early riser. I can hear the pitter patter of little
feet outside our door, shrieks of laughter, and the happy chatter of a
baby girl who's got Mimi and Papa wrapped around her little finger.

Let's dive into these two passages in Psalm 27 and Psalm 116.
Since we've been visiting my family in California, I haven't had a

regular quiet time and I *miss* my time with the Lord. Also, I am way nicer to my family when I've started my day with the cleansing Word. On this trip, we've been having some pretty serious conversations about Pete switching careers to move into sales, which is much riskier than his bread and butter job as a consultant. Even though I desperately want him to enjoy his work, I'm nervous about the financial unpredictability of a sales role. Every time we talk about it, I feel a little anxious whirring start up in my chest and I've been having some serious back-and-forth with the Lord on this topic.

Last night, Pete and I wrapped ourselves in blankets, grabbed hot mugs of coffee, and headed down to the dock to watch the twinkling stars populate the velvety night sky. The sky here is outrageously gorgeous, completely unsullied, and a profound reminder that God sits enthroned above and the heavens are his footstool. As we gently rocked in the boat, I whispered to God, "Please God, I'm having a hard time trusting you even though you have been so good to us. Can you send me a shooting star?" Sometimes, I pray like a five-year old girl, but that's ok, because Jesus encouraged us to have faith like little children. The fact that I exclusively want to dress like a five-year old girl in polka dots and tutus is another matter.

A few minutes later, the most incredible shooting star I've ever seen catapulted across the night sky. Blazing blue and orange with a fiery white tail, it swept across our view like one of those proposal banners behind an airplane, saying, "I see you, Natalie. I hear you. I am faithful."

This morning, I opened my Bible to Psalm 116 and the Lord gifted me with the verse above, Psalm 116:7–9, "Be at rest once more, O my soul, for the Lord has been good to you." He then reminded me of the last two verses of Psalm 27. Psalm 27 has long been a favorite Psalm in our family. My mentor read Psalm 27 at our wedding, and I had the privilege of reading it at a dear friend's wedding a few weeks ago. The last two verses contain one of the loveliest declarations of faith and confidence in Scripture:

> I am still confident of this: I will see the goodness of the Lord in the land of the living. Wait for the Lord; be strong and take heart and wait for the Lord. (Psalm 27:13–14)

The psalmist is confident he will see the goodness of the Lord *in the land of the living*. This phrase stands out to me because it declares the goodness of the Lord in the here and now, in our flesh and blood families, in the messy physicality of our life here on earth. Somehow I find it easier yet less compelling to envision the goodness of the Lord in heaven, once Jesus has come back and eradicated sin, and we're all together for eternity (I realize there's some work to be done on my joyful expectation of heaven). Of course we will see the goodness of the Lord in heaven, but most days that feels a long way away and I long to see his goodness here and now.

That's why I love Psalm 27. I love the promise of seeing God's goodness in my life here on earth. The psalmist knows that he will see the goodness of the Lord *in the land of the living*, and because of that confidence, he exhorts himself and future generations to do three things: (1) wait for the Lord; (2) be strong and take heart, and (3) wait for the Lord. Note that waiting for the Lord is so important that he says it twice.

Psalm 27 speaks of confident expectation, faithful courage, and advises the cultivation of a strong and resolute heart while waiting on the Lord.

Psalm 116: 7–9 picks up the same phrase, "in the land of the living," but focuses instead, on remembering God's completed acts of goodness. The psalmist is reminding himself that the Lord has been good to him, and he encourages both himself and us to find rest in that remembering.

Be at rest *once more*, O my soul, for the Lord has been good to you. For you, O lord, have delivered my soul from death, my eyes from tears, my feet from stumbling, that I may walk before the Lord in the land of the living (Psalm 116:7–9)(emphasis mine).

Here, the psalmist isn't just waiting on the goodness of the Lord in the land of the living, he is *re-living* the goodness of the Lord in the land of the living.

The phrase that jumps out at me in the passage is "once more." The psalmist says, "Be at rest *once more*, O my soul," indicating the need for a reorientation of his soul. Perhaps he too was feeling an anxious whirring in his chest and said, "Wait a minute. Be at rest once more, O my soul. I need to remember that God has been good to me." The psalmist then recounts God's goodness: (1) God delivered my soul from death; (2) he dried my tears and comforted me (Psalm 34:18); and (3) God kept my feet from stumbling. Ephesians 2:10 and Psalm 18:36 elaborate on these promises—God has a path for us and he will broaden it beneath our feet so our ankles do not turn. God grants us salvation, dries the tears from our eyes, and keeps our feet from stumbling.

He picks us up and sets us on the path he has for us, so that we may "walk before the Lord in the land of the living." He has done it before and he will do it again. He is unendingly faithful.

He has provided over and over and over again throughout my life. Even though new challenges can make me feel off kilter, he calls me to remember all the other times he has provided. He asks me to remember his character and his covenantal love for me. God has already shown me his goodness in the land of the living. Because of his faithfulness and his provision, I can be strong and take heart as our family enters uncharted territory. My soul can "be at rest once more" because I can look back and see God's loving and gracious hand of provision.

Wherever you are, whether you're feeling centered or there's an anxious whirring in your chest, take a moment to look back on the ways the Lord has provided for you. As you recall his faithfulness, may your soul "be at rest once more."

"Be strong and take heart and wait for the Lord" (Psalm 27:14).

You Will Go Out in Joy and Be Led Forth in Peace

You will go out in joy and be led forth in peace; the mountains and hills will burst into song before you, and all the trees of the field will clap their hands. (Isaiah 55:12)

Answer me quickly, Lord; my spirit fails. Do not hide your face from me or I will be like those who go down to the pit. Let the morning bring me word of your unfailing love, for I have put my trust in you. (Psalm 143:7–8)

I set the Lord always before me, because he is at my right hand, I will not be shaken. (Psalm 16:8)

… Christ loved the church and gave himself up for her to make her holy, cleansing her by the washing with water through the word. (Ephesians 5:26)

It's been six months since that special day in the cemetery when God told me to work and relish. I'm sitting on my front porch, sipping coffee, contemplating my faithful gingko tree. The first hint of fall is in the air, lending a crisp, autumn quality to the morning. The mosquitoes haven't gotten the memo yet. The thirsty bloodsuckers are swarming, emitting a high-pitched whine as they prepare to feast on my ankles.

I'm glad I listened to the Lord's kind voice that day in the cemetery because now everything in my life is changing. Next to my gingko, a small moving POD is parked. Eight years of friendships, firsts, and finding ourselves is reduced to boxes, packing tape, and sharpies. We're finishing a chapter and beginning a new one.

I've wanted to move back to California since the moment I set foot in Chicago for college. Twelve years later, this not-so-secret dream is becoming a reality. About a year ago, we started praying and fasting regularly, and it's astonishing to see how the Lord answered our prayers. He said yes to California in a surprising way, changing my husband's heart, finding him a new job, and telling him it was time to move.

For a long time, the desire to move to California had been an idol for me. A few years ago, our dear friends Ben and Abbey were praying through this matter with us. The Lord gave Abbey a beautiful picture of my dream to move home. In it, I was holding a lovely vase (moving to California) in a vise-like grip. Both of my hands were clenched tightly around it, but the Lord was asking me to release the vase into his hands. He wasn't asking me to let it shatter on the ground; he was asking me to entrust our future and our location to him. I laid it down (painfully), unsure if he would ever let me pick it back up again.

Finally, three years later, we're going home. The house is empty, the goodbyes are mostly said, and we are leaving on a jet plane.

This transition has been bittersweet for many reasons, and incredibly revelatory of some deep things in my character that I think the Lord is inviting me to work on with him.

Revelation #1:

Transition + Feelings + Meta Feelings = Emotional Upheaval

I'm a pre-processor and I hate transition. I like to feel all the feelings ahead of time, so that when I get where I'm going, I can be present for the experience, good or bad. Thus, I began mourning our move and the inevitable accompanying difficulties the second we decided it was time.

Goodness, what a rush of feelings. Relief, joy, despair, loneliness, worry, stress. Everything flooded over me, almost immediately. If you've never accomplished a cross-country move, it's a pain in the tail and *not* a good time to experience an onslaught of emotion.

First, the whole gamut of emotions swept over me. Next, the "feelings about my feelings" kicked in—the "meta feelings" (appropriately coined by my brilliant friend Hayley). I started feeling bad about all my feelings, wondering why I was so bent out of shape over a good thing.

On the morning of a small goodbye gathering, she looked me in the eye and perfectly, almost clairvoyantly, diagnosed the disorder in my soul. "You're angry with yourself for all your feelings. You're frustrated that this whole thing is throwing you out of whack in a way you can't control, especially since it's the fulfillment of something you've always wanted. It's fine to feel all the feelings, but go ahead and drop the meta feelings, ok?"

After our conversation, I started getting a little better, but let me tell you, the enemy *did not* want us to "go out in joy and be lead forth in peace." So many things during the move went wrong, or were extra expensive or frustrating. Our house didn't sell right away (and still hasn't sold at the time of writing this).

The fulfillment of my dream was certainly more work and much more complicated than I had anticipated. To combat these frustrations and, as a matter of survival, I got serious about speaking (out loud) Scripture over myself, putting on the armor of God (daily), declaring his truth over our family.

Faith is about seeing *through* our circumstances to trust God. Feelings are powerful emotions but *they are not reality.* If we rely on our visible circumstances to procure hope, we will undoubtedly be discouraged. Thankfully, our Heavenly Father owns the whole spectrum, the earthly realm *and* the spiritual realm. That's why prayer is absolutely critical, especially when circumstances are shaky and uncertain. Prayer both grounds us and gives us certainty in the faithfulness of God and his character. We may not know exactly *how* he will choose to answer our prayers, but the process of prayer, particularly the exercise of praying scripture, builds our faith. Through prayer, we become unswervingly convinced of his goodness to us, even when circumstances seem to belie this reality. Psalm 143:7–8:

> Answer me quickly, Lord; my spirit fails. Do not hide your face from me or I will be like those who go down to the pit. Let the morning bring me word of your unfailing love, for I have put my trust in you.

Revelation #2:
We Are Always Longing for Something

Do you ever get so sick of yourself? Do you wish you could just turn your brain off and stop being confronted, every waking hour of the day, with your own frailty and lame tendencies? I sure do!

My mind is like a hamster wheel, always going, going, going. At any given moment, I'm thinking about 7,500 different things, overanalyzing social interactions, and planning for future events unlikely to occur. It's exhausting to be inside my head.

I love to ask people, when there's a slight lull in conversation, "Hey, what are you thinking about?" Men love this, right? Every time I ask my husband this question, he always says, "Nothing." Since I possess such an overactive mind I thought surely, he must be fibbing. He just doesn't want to tell me.

Finally, years into our marriage, he said, "Natalie, I promise you, I am not thinking about anything. My mind is a like a giant blank white board, a tabula rasa. This is my natural state of being. If I want to think about anything, it takes a good deal of conscious effort to make something come onto that blank slate."

I stared at him, utterly gobsmacked. Your mind is a blank slate? You're truly not thinking about anything in there? What is that like? That sounds so peaceful!

One of the recurrent thoughts on the hamster wheel of my mind is a faint disgust with myself for immediately replacing my longing to move to California with new longings.

Moving to California has looked a little different than I expected. I thought we would sell our house in DC for a nice profit, buy a cute little home in California, and maybe even attempt a remodel. I pictured my husband sallying forth each day to a fulfilling and financially stable job.

Reality check. Our house is still for sale, we are living with my parents, and we accepted a job he really likes, but it involves a strong element of financial unpredictability and our finances may not stabilize for some time. Yikes! Definitely not what I had in mind. In many ways, this move feels like a step back, and in some ways, it is. Yet we're believing that this transition will lead to a life-giving career for Pete and a family set-up that makes the most sense for us in the long run.

Back to replacing my longings—after the Lord said yes to California, did I spend weeks and months high on a mountaintop, praising and thanking him for giving me the desire of my heart? Did I finally enter the land of contentment never to want for anything again? No. Because I'm a fickle-hearted creature "prone to wander, Lord, I feel it. Prone to leave the God I love …"[10]

Here's what I would like to say happened: as soon as the longing for California was fulfilled, I was immediately satisfied and spent our final five weeks in DC on cloud nine, unperturbed by the mere exigencies of moving.

Unfortunately, my fickle heart kicked into stability-craving overdrive. Like a swift locomotive hurtling down the train tracks, my mind clicked onto another longing track, replacing my longing for California with longings for my own home, for a stable income, a posse of new friends, another baby. Sheesh, I'm the worst.

Thankfully, I don't serve a God who thinks I'm the worst. He meets me in my frailty, in my complicated emotions, in my longing. We sit together and examine everything. We sift the good from the bad, the worthy from the unworthy. He shows me what to do with my longing.

We are created for complete unity with God. Since the Fall introduced sin and separation from God, we have become creatures of longing, creatures of waiting. We long for heaven, for eternity, for permanent reconciliation with God. As we await Christ's victorious return, this fundamental facet of our humanity becomes either a prime tool in the enemy's toolbox or a valuable asset for our ongoing sanctification.

So here's what I'm thinking about as I consider my longing. I'm attempting to reconcile my longing with the need to practice contentment, whatever my circumstances. If I'm always longing for something, what does it look like to wait well? What does it look like to trust God? How do I look toward the future with confident hope instead of anxiety? I think it looks like prayer and release. Persistent, fervent asking, followed by a calm assurance. I'm also expanding my

---

[10]   Robert Robinson (text) John Wyeth Nettleton (melody). "Come, Thou Fount of Every Blessing." 1757.

asking beyond the specifics of my physical needs—I'm asking him to protect my heart and mind. I'm asking him for faith. I need power, through the Holy Spirit, to trust. Trust is not my natural response, but that doesn't have to be my forever story. Our longing can lead us astray or it can lead us to the author and perfecter of our faith. I choose the latter and my hope is that you will too.

Revelation #3:
I Think Everything is Hard.

A few weeks before leaving DC, I had dinner with my dear friend, law school compatriot, and trusted editor, Bex. Over spicy crunchy tuna and crispy egg rolls we gave each other the rundown of our respective emotional states. Bex is not into overly emotional displays of religiosity or pat Christian phrases. Naturally, I love to ask her, in all seriousness, "How's your heart?" Even though she mocks me, we answer the question because it's worthy of being answered.

That evening I was, of course, awash with emotion. With tears and halting phrases, I unloaded in the way you can only unload with an old and trusted friend.

Finally, in a massive roundaboutation (not a word, but should be a word), I finally said out loud, "I think everything is hard." I stopped for a second there, and realized with more than a little chagrin, that I *do* think everything is hard. Ugh. That being said, even by my low standards, moving is rough.

Here's the rub: ninety-percent of adult life is hard. It's especially daunting if you're the kind of person who thinks that everything that is not sitting on a beach, reading a novel, sipping a G&T is hard. And I think everything that is not vacation is hard.

You know those people who jump out of bed in the morning, full of energy and vigor, ready to deal with life and all its unpredictability?

They thrive on accomplishing to-do lists, executing tasks, and being upstanding, competent humans. Yeah, I'm not one of those.

Every single thing I do, every day, I do because it stands between me and me reading an excellent novel in my bed. Seriously. That's the only reason I do anything, because I have to do it, so that I can get back to reading a novel in my bed.

If my natural habitat is reading a novel in bed, then it's unsurprising that I think almost everything else is challenging. Also, it took me thirty years to realize this. What a joke!

I long to be one of those people who just do life things like it's no big deal. Almost all of my friends are that way—super competent, unflappable, high-capacity, you know the type.

Well, in an announcement that will surprise no except myself, I am not that way.

When I first realized this unhappy truth about myself, I thought, "Ah, my way is clear. I must learn how to suck it up and not complain about the things that everyone else does without complaining. I will wow them with my competence. Nothing will stress me out. I will become unflappable." Then I became very tired at the thought of trying to live this way and just further contemplated the comfort of my bed and a good book.

Thus, I rapidly abandoned this line of thinking because it sounded like a lot of work. Now I've slowly come to terms with this revelation about myself. I'm probably not going to become a different, more capable person overnight. I can, however, know this tendency about myself and not be overcome by it.

When stress and worry and frustration over basic (very basic) life tasks begin to overwhelm me, I'm learning to take a minute. I'm realizing that these feelings will pass, the task will be accomplished (because it stands between me and reading my novel in bed), and the sky is not falling.

Revelation #4:

I Want to Be a Woman of Peace.

I Thessalonians 5:23 says, "May God himself, the God of peace, sanctify you through and through. May your whole spirit, soul and body be kept blameless at the coming of our Lord Jesus Christ. The one who calls you is faithful and he will do it."

It's so interesting that the God of *peace* is sanctifying. Peace and sanctification seem like they would be unhappy bedfellows. But Ephesians 2:14 says, "He himself is our peace." God is a God of peace. He is faithful and *he will sanctify us through and through.*

Because we've been together on this journey for a while, it's no surprise to you that I'm always craving a circumstantial peace. A circumstantial peace is not a peace worthy of pursuit. A peace that's blown to and fro by the shifting wind? Precarious at best. A peace that's easily overcome by slight changes of plan? Not really worth having, right?

But an enduring peace? A peace that rises above? That kind of peace is worthy of pursuit. I want that kind of peace to suffuse my entire body. I want peace that positively oozes out of my pores, making me tranquil, assured, steadfast.

How do we get that kind of peace? I wish I could say I've got it 24/7, no problem. I don't, unfortunately, but I can tell you that the Lord is working on it in my heart. I don't know what the entire process looks like. But I do know, in the depths of my soul, in the marrow of my bones, where to begin.

In. The. Word. Of. God.

A lasting peace comes through intimacy with Jesus. An enduring peace comes through knowledge of his character, which is found in his Word. To become women of peace, we practice and fail, but we persist. We lose our cool and try again. But we never stop trying. We keep pursuing peace that transcends circumstances. To grow, we have to build our faith muscles. We have to practice. Practice is diligence in prayer. Practice is learning the Word of God so that when the enemy attacks your thoughts, or life throws you a curve ball, the first thing that comes to your mind is truth. Practice isn't fun, but it matters, it counts, it works.

Here's what practice looked like recently when I started losing it about our financial situation. We just moved to a ridiculously expensive area, we are living with my parents, our house has not sold, my husband took a serious pay cut in what feels like a risky new job, medical, insurance, and car expenses keep cropping up, and it feels like we are bleeding capital. These circumstances are compounded by the fact that everyone around me appears to be incredibly wealthy with beautiful homes, sparkly diamonds, fancy cars, and fancy gym bodies to prove it. Now that we know each other well, this sounds like a perfect storm for me, right?

As I am wont to do, I started having a meltdown (on the inside), totally freaking out that we are never going to be able to make it here. Our current situation has activated some old hang-ups about money, security, and success, so as my freak-out-o-meter started rising, I knew I was dealing with some heavy historical baggage. A few days into this meltdown, just as my husband and I were trying to get out of the house to go on a hike, I hit my limit. Alone upstairs, I started crying in the bathroom, tired of these stupid old hang-ups, worried about the future, and frustrated with my freak out-prone self.

Thankfully, I am not the same woman I was three years ago when I began this journey with the Lord. He has taught me a thing or two about dealing with the enemy, the one who loves to whisper lies and discouragement in our ears. It was time for some lie replacement therapy. I made us late for our hike, but it was time well spent.

I sat down with a notebook and wrote out the following lies I believe about wealth:

- Being rich will make me safe.

- Being rich will mean I have arrived (whatever that means).
- Being rich will mean I never have to worry.
- Being rich means I did something right and I didn't miss an opportunity.

Then I wrote out God's truth underneath every lie, using what he says about himself in his Word.

- Being rich will make me safe.
  - Only God can make me safe. "The name of the Lord is a strong tower; the righteous [woman] runs into it and is safe" (Proverbs 18:10 ESV). "After this, the word of the Lord came to Abram in a vision: 'Do not be afraid, Abram. I am your shield, your very great reward'" (Genesis 15:1).
- Being rich will mean I have arrived (whatever that means).
  - God knows the plans he has for me (Jeremiah 29:11) and my "arrival" with him is the only thing that matters, both on this earth and in eternity. "But the Lord said to Samuel, 'Do not consider his appearance or his height, for I have rejected him. The Lord does not look at the things people look at. People look at the outward appearance, but the Lord looks at the heart'" (1 Samuel 16:7).
- Being rich will mean I never have to worry.
  - My status as a daughter of the Creator of the universe is what means I never have to worry. God is my father, and he loves to give me good gifts (Matthew 7:11). He owns the cattle on a thousand hills (Psalm 50:10). Moreover, he tells me not to worry about what I will wear or what I will eat, because he knows my needs (Matthew 6:25-34). One of the names of God, Jehovah Jireh, means "The Lord Will Provide" (Genesis 22:14). If the Lord

will provide for me, I do not need to worry, whether I'm wealthy or not.

- Being rich means I did something right and I didn't miss an opportunity.
  o The Lord knows the plans he has for me and they are good plans (Jeremiah 29:11). These plans may or may not include wealth, but I can rest assured that he has prepared good works in advance for me to do (Ephesians 2:10). If I'm never wealthy, it does not mean I did something wrong or missed an opportunity. "Many are the plans in a person's heart, but it is the Lord's purpose that prevails" (Proverbs 19:21). "No one can serve two masters. Either you will hate the one and love the other, or you will be devoted to the one and despise the other. You cannot serve both God and money" (Matthew 6:24). I want to serve God, not money.

After this exercise, I felt a lot better. Once you take the time to concretely identify the lies you believe, it's a lot easier to defeat them with the truth of Scripture. James 4:7 says, "resist the devil, and he will flee from you." Lie replacement therapy is resisting the devil. Declaring the truth of God (to ourselves) shuts up the enemy and kicks him to the curb. You may be facing a different set of lies, but I promise you, with whatever set of lies you believe, there are truths in the Word of God to refute them. You are a holy and dearly loved daughter of the King. The enemy has *nothing* on you. Your life was redeemed at a price, the price of Jesus' death on the cross for your sins. You are called by God, you are loved by God, and you are kept safe by God (Jude 1:1). Your citizenship is in heaven and no one, Satan included, can ever take that away from you. Don't give up your peace freely. Fight for it with the Word of God. Press in for peace in your heart and in your mind. Press in for peace in your homes, in your families, and in your relationships. It will not be easy, Jesus himself said, "in this world you will have trouble, but take heart, I have *overcome* the world" (John 16:33). Don't give up. Persevere.

Since moving to California, we've encountered a lot of difficult situations that are chomping at the bit to steal our peace. We have an income we can't survive on (without living with my parents) that may not grow sufficiently for a year or more. Our house in DC fell out of escrow twice in five days (over Thanksgiving). A thousand other super irritating details went wrong with insurance providers, cell phone providers, doctor's offices, etc. It seems as if everything that could be challenging has been challenging. I'm not going to lie, I've done my fair share of freaking out and feeling overwhelmed with this transition, *but* becoming a woman of peace is the practice I keep coming back to. It's the prayer of my heart. My prayers are often jumbled and stressed, but I press in, asking the Lord, "Please, make me a woman of peace. Help me to be a woman of peace." And then I wait in confident expectation for his provision of peace because I know it is his will for me and mine.

When I was pregnant with Penny, the Lord gave me a verse to pray over her. Isaiah 26:3-4 says, "He will keep in perfect peace, [her] whose heart is steadfast because [she] trusts in him. Trust in the Lord forever, for the Lord, the Lord himself, is the Rock eternal." When we trust in him, our hearts are steadfast. When we exercise our trust muscles, our steadfast hearts are kept in perfect peace. Not half peace, not sort of peace. *Perfect* peace.

There are lots of books about God and many of them are worthy of your time. But there is only one book *by* God about himself. Open the Bible, start at the beginning, start in the middle, it doesn't really matter, just start somewhere. Try adding a Psalm every day because it's good for your soul. Some days, it may only be a verse or a phrase, but carry it with you, roll it over on your tongue, let it percolate through your mind.

"Now may the Lord of peace himself give you peace at all times and in every way. The Lord be with all of you" (2 Thessalonians 3:16).

I leave you with this encouragement, "… Christ loved the church and gave himself up for her to make her holy, cleansing her by the washing with water through the word" (Ephesians 5:26).

He loves you.

He gave himself up for you.

He makes you holy.

He cleanses you by washing you with water through the Word.

Printed in the United States
By Bookmasters